C000216621

Wabi Sabi
for Writers

Find Inspiration.

Respect Imperfection.

Create Peerless Beauty.

Richard R. Powell

Adams Media

Avon, Massachusetts

Copyright © 2006 CWL Publishing Enterprises, Inc.
This is a CWL Publishing Enterprises book developed for Adams Media by
CWL Publishing Enterprises, Inc., Madison, Wisconsin, *www.cwlpub.com.*
All rights reserved. This book, or parts thereof, may not be reproduced in
any form without permission from the publisher; exceptions are made for
brief excerpts used in published reviews.

Published by Adams Media, an F+W Publications Company
57 Littlefield Street
Avon, MA 02322
www.adamsmedia.com

ISBN: 1-59337-596-4
Printed in Canada.
J I H G F E D C B A

Library of Congress Cataloging-in-Publication Data
Powell, Richard R.
Wabi sabi for writers / Richard R. Powell.
p.   cm.
Includes bibliographical references
ISBN 1-59337-596-4
1. Authorship--Psychological aspects. 2. Wabi. 3. Sabi. I. Title.
PN171.P83P69 2006
808'.02019--dc22
2006005205

This publication is designed to provide accurate and authoritative information with regard to the subject matter covered. It is sold with the understanding that the publisher is not engaged in rendering legal, accounting, or other
professional advice. If legal advice or other expert assistance is required, the
services of a competent professional person should be sought.
   —From a *Declaration of Principles* jointly adopted by a Committee of the
American Bar Association and a Committee of Publishers and Associations

Many of the designations used by manufacturers and sellers to distinguish
their product are claimed as trademarks. Where those designations appear in
this book and Adams Media was aware of a trademark claim, the designations have been printed with initial capital letters.

This book is available at quantity discounts for bulk purchases.
For information, please call 1-800-872-5627.

Dedication

To Marilyn and our literary life together

Acknowledgments

Thanks to: Marilyn for her ongoing help and support; Matthew and Graham, who gave their dad time to write; Ron and the Wednesday night group for thoughtful input; the Board of Directors at ICCS and my colleagues who supported me and took on extra work so I could concentrate on this project. Special thanks to Michael Jewell, who encouraged me to write from the heart; John Woods of CWL Publishing Enterprises for his wise direction; Kate Epstein, Meredith O'Hayre, Kate Petrella, and the team at Adams Media for shining editorial and production work; Dr. Lynken Ghose for sending me his article *A Study in Buddhist Psychology: Is Buddhism Truly Pro-Detachment and Anti-Attachment?*; and the thirty-three writers and readers who filled out the *Still in the Stream* (*www.stillinthestream.com*) readers' survey. Additional thanks to the librarians and library staff who helped me with resources, and to the authors who exemplify and model wabi sabi writing: Basho (and his translators), David Macfarlane, Anne Michaels, Carol Shields, E. Annie Proulx, Annie Dillard, Bailey White, Norman Maclean, Mark Haddon, Robert M. Pirsig, Thomas Merton, Walter Wangerin, C. S. Lewis, Frederick Buechner, Robert Farrar Capon, and many haiku poets too numerous to name.

Contents

Preface

The corner of Georgia and Howe in downtown Vancouver. Tall steel and glass buildings create wind that drives grit against pedestrians. Towers like these also produce word storms that swirl out across assorted media. Jingles designed to catch like burrs in mind fabric tumble in the squall; slogans engineered to stick to neural fibers flap and glow and blink. Advertisers compete to pierce our jargon-armor with sharp couplets. On streets like this I dry up. Hollow catch-phrases wither me; I'm buried in the scorching dross of brain scams: Diamonds Are Forever . . . It's the Cheesiest . . . Have It Your Way . . . Fly the Friendly Skies . . . You Deserve a Break Today . . . Got Milk? . . . Leave the Driving to Us . . . The One That Lasts . . . Think Different . . . You Got the Right One Baby . . . Oh What a Feeling.

The feeling is a vacuum: parched, desiccated, and empty. In this maelstrom of snappy one-liners I am illiterate, unable to decipher, overwhelmed with polish. I long to leave lingo and enter language. I thirst for liquid locution; hunger for nutritious narrative. I want text that connects. And this longing draws me into community with other readers, weaves me into a tapestry of text addicts, a society of story lovers.

Authors who produce writing with substance have an almost sacred role in the word-worn world. They are priests of poetry, prophets of perspective. Their writing is ingested, digested, and integrated. A sacrament of words. A consumption of concepts.

Why is this writing invited in while others are cast out? Because this writing waters idea seeds with the fresh rain of attention.

Are you called to write like this? Do you want to take readers beyond themselves into a trembling grove of wabi sabi, where they can drink from a hidden spring? This book will help you open that spring in the mountain of your days. It will open with a set of ancient Japanese principles that gave the first novel ever written a unique and lasting freshness. Those principles continue to guide the most read and written form of poetry today. This book shows you the "Way of Elegance," a path that leads to a deep understanding of wabi sabi and a deeper expression of it in your writing.

On the Way of Elegance, you are an archaeologist of each moment. With pen or pixel you pierce the ground of being and dig up artifacts of awareness. By uncovering these bones of beauty you will free narrative, and the narrative will carry you forward into the coiled run-out of letters on a page. You will fill pages with savings, the things worth saving, and they will be living lanterns lit with luminescent words. From those pages readers' brains will sparkle. You know the kind I mean—you have read them before. They glow with something beyond human effort; they outshine the author; they take readers beyond themselves. Wabi sabi is for writers. It will help your writing shine.

THE LAST FERRY HOME
HER FOOD GROWS COLD
WHILE SHE READS

One

Wabi Sabi for Writers:
an introduction

THE OLD SCHOOL

SAME FLOOR WAX

DIFFERENT KIDS

雁

The Tenth Goose

Nine Canada geese lift off a clear mountain lake; droplets from their wings cast lines of rings behind them on the glassy surface as they rise. Light gray feathers reflect amber light from the early morning sun, a clean glow off each curved body. You watch their broad wings grip air, watch nine bodies rise and fall in rhythm against the dark forest behind them. Each bird's neck kinks in counter-time to its wing beats so that all nine heads remain level and each set of eyes gazes steadily out at the cool dawn, bright mystery of sight amid the shiny black head feathers. Closer now, you make out the expressionless curve of their beaks, see one goose's thin moist tongue as she honks; hear the whistle of air across wing feathers as they pass over your head. Then you notice that there is a tenth goose far back, low to the water, working hard to catch up, honking softly, as if each wing beat hurts. This goose loses a feather as she passes close over you and you watch the feather spiral and glide to the ground. You pick it up and it looks perfect, each barbule lying neatly against its neighbor, the tiny whorl of fluff near the calamus soft to the touch. Then you see that the shaft is not perfect; it is cracked open from the middle to the tip.

You keep that feather, tuck it under the strap around your car's sun visor, look at it every day you drive to work and remember the tenth goose. Remember your own efforts to keep up. And somehow, that tenth goose gives you courage. You wonder if she will find enough food or if winter will separate her from the rest, separate her from life. She speaks to you in a dream one night. In the distracted moments of the day she speaks to you, in the elevator or while you wait in traffic. Then one night she is there in your dream again, as silent as her feather in your car. She tips her head at you and that beak, with its lumpy prominence like a Roman nose, bobs up and down and you realize she is giving you permission to speak. In the dream you speak and she turns her head to hear you and you tell her your fear of dying and your hopes while living and she comes and rattles her beak between your fingers. Her hard lips silently mouth the ancient words "wabi sabi" and then she is gone and a snowflake melts on your hand and leaves a small cold drop the size of a tear.

The First Important Thing

The tenth goose is beautiful. There is energy in her story that returns to beauty inside a reader like water returns to a snowflake inside winter clouds. If you manage to tell the story right that goose with all her wisdom emerges alive and radiant inside another human being. You can tell her story a hundred ways, over and over again, because it doesn't have to be about a goose. It is about a beauty that we never grow tired of looking at. Do you get tired of looking at a forest in spring? Do you say, "I've seen that already; those green leaves bursting from their buds are something I never want to see again"? How about a beautiful sunset? Have you seen enough in your lifetime? When you are driving home at the end of a day and a great bright orange glow floods over your face, can you resist looking up? Can you keep yourself from exclaiming with wonder as the orange hot ball of light descends beyond the ocean's curve?

Wabi sabi beauty tumbles out of ordinary life; your ordinary life or your family's or your friend's or your fellow worker's or the little neighbor boy who brings you a broken shell from the stream, just like that, just to look at. "I want it back," he says, "but you can hold it," and your job at that moment is to just admire it. Comment on the color, look him in the eye and let him know that you understand what it is like to find a shell in the cold water of the stream as beautiful as a jewel. You can also feel that great inner sadness that a child will not usually know, that the clam that made that shell is gone, the crayfish that ate the shell clean is gone, and the heron that ate the crayfish has flown away. This is part of the story that the little boy may not know. It is part of the story you may not know. But one day that little boy will see the heron at the creek eating a crayfish and another day he will see a crayfish eating from a broken shell, and one day the boy will put it all together and one day, maybe, he will grasp the great chain of things that swirl around us in an ever-changing pattern. And also—and this is the first important wabi sabi thing I have to tell you—one day he will forget. Part of the job of a writer who knows and loves wabi sabi is to remind others of what they already know but have forgotten, just like the feather in your car.

It is a strange delight to find that you can tell a story about a wabi sabi feather or shell or the event around it and that story unfolds its energy inside your reader to reveal the same wisdom that is buried in every ordinary life. It may mean that you simply tell what you don't yet know, describe an image or moment that you know is large and important. You may not have a word for the emotion you feel. Write something else in its place, but go on and paint a picture of the ordinary mysteries. Your life will teach you which stories to tell and which details to notice. If you are faithful to the story, if you develop your intuition, prick up your ears, look for the telling details, the detail worth telling, you will be able to condense it all down into wabi sabi words filled with beauty. Then your reader will love you for telling what is real and authentic and moving. Because the truth is that sometimes in life we are the lead goose strong and sure, and sometimes we are in the flock taking our place, and sometimes we are way behind straining to catch up, and sometimes we are standing on the shore of a lake taking it all in and finding a feather in it. When you hold that feather you are a wabi sabi watcher, and when you move from seeing to writing what you see, you are a wabi sabi writer.

What is it about the beauty of that feather that is so important? Here is the answer: It is a kind of beauty on the edge of defeat, a beauty tenacious and brave, and it is the beauty left behind when the warm, honking goose is gone. And not just flown away—but dead and gone. That feather remains as a testament to the beauty in living, and even when the feather dries and cracks and is eventually eaten by insects or the drab extension of time, it will live on in the imaginations of those who hear the story of the tenth goose. I have given it to you because you have taken the time to read this book. One day the goose and the feather and the image in a warm human imagination will all be gone, and the wonderful mystery is that the beauty will still remain. The beauty of that feather is not necessarily the greatest and not necessarily the least kind of beauty. But it is a kind of beauty that connects you, attaches you to something bigger, something deeper, something older than you are. It pulses like wing beats, drums like hoof beats, snaps like sail sheets in the moment the boat turns to tack. It is a beauty that changes; it is a beauty that grows. You may find yourself trailing after it like an old man trails after his wife of sixty years. You may find yourself standing with it while the throng moves around you. You may find yourself captivated by it in something as small as three blades of grass, greener than they should be, there in the crack of the concrete parking lot. Is it worth noticing? Worth sharing? Are there words to describe it? Go ahead and try; words will not diminish it. Words are like grass pushing up where you least expect them. Words are gifts. Let them grow.

What Is Wabi Sabi?

The definition of the Japanese words *wabi sabi* has changed over the years. At one time when the Japanese language was young, *wabi* meant "poverty," and *sabi* meant "loneliness." During the first major flowering of Japanese culture, *wabi* came to refer to the ideal hermit's life, lived in contemplation of nature and appreciation of the spiritual and aesthetic values underlying a solitary existence. His was a wabi way. The Japanese tea masters of the fifteenth and sixteenth centuries developed a wabi style of tea ceremony as an alternative to the ornate and ostentatious ceremony in which the aristocracy would show off their valuable tea objects and forge political alliances. *Sabi* was refined over the years to emphasize a state of receptivity, fostered in remote natural settings. This positive aloneness was joined to the wabi appreciation of the understated and unrefined to form a phrase with deep resonance for the contemplative mind. People would dream of living in simple enlightened appreciation of nature.

Then a man named Basho saw those two words and used them for a higher purpose still. He used them to express what it was he saw in all the lovely lonely moments of his life, not just the lovely lonely places. He noticed the poignant passings, the fragile wonders like snowflakes and the sound snow makes when it slumps, and the irrational happiness after he gave away something he loved. In the 300 years since Basho taught his students this deep definition for those old words, other people have taken up the process. This is what happens with a language. Each generation takes the words and uses them. Some of the words get worn out; others shiny with use; others still, practiced into something more profound, transmuted into a metal of a subtler variety.

These Japanese words are deep pools that Westerners long to dive into. Together they represent a way of being that celebrates the beauty of age, the richness of character, the importance of imperfection, and the reality of impermanence. These subjects are not easily exhausted, not easily put to logic or reason. But story can capture such beauty, can reveal such character, and can show the value of noticing imperfection and impermanence. Perhaps you are called to follow wabi sabi down into the deep waters of beauty where no goose has gone before.

The Second Important Thing

Here is the second important thing I have to tell you: Nothing is perfect, nothing lasts, nothing is finished. When you first hear this you might think, "Are you telling me my writing will never be perfect or finished and will not last?" My answer is, "Exactly." If you are writing in the hopes that your masterpiece will be perfect and everlasting, you will trail away from wabi sabi into the soundless rooms of delusion and disappointment from which few emerge until they realize their mistake. The truth is that everything changes, and that writing is only a reasonably permanent form of expression. Very few writers accomplish lasting notoriety, and the ones who do will never know the long-term effect of their work.

Writing is an exercise in polishing a beautiful stone of perception. Some of these well-turned, well-proportioned, carefully chosen stones will be collected and passed on from one generation to the next, while others will sink into the ground as part of the rich humus of culture. The reason I use the analogy of stones is that without literacy, without context, without a living culture in which the concepts and ideas of a book can breathe and evolve, the book will just be paper and ink and glue. Without literacy, a book is just an object; without a cultural context, it is just words.

What wabi sabi can do for your writing is help it age well; impart a particular kind of beauty that retains appeal over time.

How do I know this? Because I have found wabi sabi in many of the great books from years gone by. Some books are so infused with it that I venture to say they do not just contain wabi sabi elements but are in fact whole and enlightened wabi sabi books. In Chapter 2, I list a number of the books that I go back to again and again for inspiration. Wabi sabi essays, articles, short stories, novels, and other writings contain some or all of the following elements:

- Nature, including human nature, presented artistically and accurately
- Clear evocative descriptions that make you feel like you are there
- Realism or a sense that some bare and essential reality is seen
- Unique and well-developed characters who grow and change
- A sense of deep connection with a place or a time
- A feeling of authenticity
- Moments of "Aha!"
- Wonder
- Texture
- Economy of expression
- Carefully tempered erudition
- Melancholy moods and tones
- Stoic optimism
- Poetry

I come away from a wabi sabi book feeling awakened, sober, thankful, or changed. It is not escapism or fantasy; at least not *just* that. On the other hand, it is not particularly useful in the way a manual for fixing a car is. There is in these books a certain somber wisdom, but one that goes beyond nihilism, pessimism, or maudlin torpor. As with the tenth goose there is a hopeful yearning, a straining forward, a rooting for the underdog. Wabi sabi stories may be tragic, but that is not a requirement. Wabi sabi books transmit an essence; provide an uncluttered view past distractions, delusions, and expectations. When I was a boy, my father took me on wilderness treks into the mountains. We would camp beside glacier-fed lakes, and in the mornings, rising with the summer sun, we would kneel on a hard stone outcropping and reach into the icy lake with our hands and bring swift splashes of water to our own outstretched faces. What a shock that cold water was, how the lungs responded with gasps. Wabi sabi books can have the same effect. Consider the following examples:

A Partial Success

Henry David Thoreau filled thirty-nine journals with more than two million words during the course of his short life. Out of that two-million-word stream of consciousness he gleaned enough usable text for three books and a few essays. Several other works were extracted from this reservoir after his death. The first book he chose to present to the world was entitled *A Week on the Concord and Merrimack Rivers*. It was essentially self-published and sold 200 copies. The remainder of the print run collected dust on Thoreau's shelves until just before his death, when they were taken off his hands by a publisher who was interested in reprinting Thoreau's second book, *Walden*. A scant 2,000 copies of *Walden* were sold in his lifetime, but this publisher realized there was something to it that warranted a second print run.

Writing had never been Thoreau's bread and butter, a fact that saddened and disappointed him, but toward the end of his life he may have had an inkling that his words were about to fly to a much larger audience. Yet the sobering fact remains that during his lifetime he was not able to make a living as a writer. Today, we do not remember Thoreau as a pencil maker or a surveyor (the things he actually did to earn a living). We remember how his writing eventually found its audience and changed the lives of thousands of readers. Martin Luther King Jr. was one such reader, as was Ghandi. Numerous teachers through the years have pressed *Walden* knowingly into the hands of quiet thoughtful students and misunderstood rebels alike.

Thoreau's life story tells us two things. First, initial failure or lack of recognition isn't necessarily the mark of a bad writer. And second, even though the mass of humanity is complacent and placated inside their lives of quiet desperation, the message contained in Thoreau's books still speaks clearly, still calls out his authentic voice full of natural wisdom and beauty. In his work I recognize that he found a source I too am looking for. His is a stream of wisdom we all cross from time to time but only a few of us stop to drink from. Thoreau realized only partial success in his life as a writer, but his writing was a huge success in the long run.

Our Teacher

You may have heard of Thoreau, but the archetypal wabi sabi writer is a man who is less well known in the English-speaking world. His name was Basho and he lived more than 300 years ago in Japan. His students loved him, and I think you will too. There are several reasons you should get to know him if you don't already. For one thing, he was an interesting person who lived during an interesting time; for another, he knew some valuable things about writing.

Basho did something that changed the course of literary history. He took some overworked ideals and showed them to readers in a new way. He called those ideals "wabi sabi." Basho rooted around in the language and selected "wabi" and "sabi" as words suited to convey what the ideals were really all about. "I am a wabi man who has tried to know every wabi thing," Basho once said. He went on to invent haiku. That is a gross simplification, of course, but he was the first to make something of haiku that had not been made before. He made a poetic form into an avenue of enlightenment. Consequently, in this book, I will have much to say about haiku. Basho invented haiku because the form is intimate and sensual. Once you really "get it" you will never be able to go back to ordinary writing without the soft whisper of haiku in your ear.

Writing about Wabi Sabi

Some people who embrace wabi sabi do so because it expresses an ancient value system that strikes them as wholly their own.

This value system says that nonrational ways of knowing are less subject to delusion than is the artificial world of logic, reason, and conscious thought. For them, wabi sabi is a kind of enlightenment, or at the very least, a set of aesthetic principles that lead to enlightenment. Enlightenment of this sort is said to be beyond the rational mind. Koans and meditation in Zen, for instance, are ways of taking a person past the stumbling blocks of reason to pure direct apprehension of reality in its fundamental nakedness, stripped of thought structures, concepts, schemas, and established perceptions. This *dharma* (a practice that improves the quality of life) teaches that we must set aside our preconceptions and expectations of the way things are, and just look at them as directly as possible. People who hold such a view find the suggestion that wabi sabi can somehow be understood, even talked about, silly. They think it cheapens it and makes it an intellectual commodity. "Examining wabi sabi with the monkey-mind," these deeply intuitive people say, "will only cover it with concepts that get in the way." For them, concepts are intellectual constructs that fix a certain view of existence and thus limit real awareness. Wabi sabi for these folks must be nonlinguistic, must be left bigger than words, must not be reduced to sentences.

The trouble with this argument is that it is itself a line of reasoning. Rather than being something beyond reason, wabi sabi is instead its counterpart and complement.

A monk and his master set out on a pilgrimage to climb to the summit of a sacred mountain. All along the way the monk pointed to trees and flowers and vistas and cloud formations, exclaiming, "Roshi, look at that!" "Roshi, over here, see this!" "Beautiful!" "Awesome!" "Incredible!" "What a sight!" All the way the master climbed steadily, neither responding to the young man's enthusiasm nor making any comment. When at last they reached the top the monk came to stand by his master and said, "Roshi, all the way up this spectacular mountain I have been pointing out all these wonders; do you not find it all so beautiful?" The Roshi looked sternly at his young companion and replied, "Yes, but what a pity to say so."

Why is it a pity to say so? What's wrong with exclaiming with delight at the beauty of the natural world? Why should you stay silent about something that moves you? Does the Roshi's comment get at something important, or is it just the opinion of a grumpy old man? If you are going to write about wabi sabi or incorporate wabi sabi into your writing, you must contemplate the Roshi's statement.

Is it that language is inadequate to the task? Or is it that describing beauty takes something away from it? Or is it that engaging the part of the mind that is involved in language takes away from the experience of appreciation? Or is there some other reason for not commenting, for not pointing out, for not verbalizing your love of beauty?

The Third Most Important Thing

One thing I have learned from the Roshi is that our efforts to share wabi sabi with our readers must be tempered with a genuine respect for silence and the careful and judicious use of language. This is not to say that it can't be talked about, thought about, written about, and applied. What it means is that you must be diligent to develop a respectful intuition for it. You can reach a place in your life where wabi sabi is so mindfully integrated into your value system that you will write from a comfort with things as they are. There is a quiet satisfaction when wabi sabi is woven so completely into your life that you no longer have to think about it; you simply live it. And here is the third important thing I have to tell you. Wabi sabi is a way of living that is particularly conducive to writing. It will impel you to write.

To help us find our way through the maze of intuition and aesthetic appreciation that may seem daunting to a person new to wabi sabi, I will be enlisting Basho's help. As the man who redefined wabi sabi more than three centuries ago and did something in his own writing that influenced the way countless writers have gone about their craft down to this day, he is our most qualified guide. What Shakespeare did with English, Basho did with Japanese. He learned all the old stories, poems, and great works of literature and then used that wealth of knowledge to create masterpieces of prose and poetry that beguile us with their simplicity and beauty.

You will find dialogues with Basho at the beginning of each chapter. They contain a mixture of the actual teachings of Basho, my own paraphrases of Basho's ideas, and some creative license. I hope this intimate dialogue with the master wabi sabi writer of all time will reveal the depth of the subject in a creative way. Here is a short exchange to get us started.

Writer: "Hello Basho."

Basho: "Aha! I am awake. Have I recovered from my illness or is this another life?"

Writer: "Neither. I re-created you as a literary device so you can teach us about writing."

Basho: "I am reduced to a literary device? Some sort of puppet teacher? Well, I suppose that is fitting. In my life people would not leave me alone but insisted that I teach them."

Writer: "We hope you will now help us with the kind of writing we want to do."

Basho: "What kind of writing is that?"

Writer: "We want our writing to contain depth, to astonish readers with beauty, to satisfy readers with texture, and to touch readers with authentic stories. We want our writing to be wabi sabi."

Basho: "Oh, the hardest kind of writing. Well, you are ambitious, if nothing else."

Writer: "Why is wabi sabi writing the hardest?"

Basho: "Try too hard and it is gone. Like hurrying to finish meditation, like chipping a tea cup to make it more beautiful, like painting a flower onto the petal of a flower. If you hurry wabi sabi, it withers; if you manipulate it, it feels contrived; if you force it, it looks cheap. No one can take a morning glory that is stretched across a garden path and arrange it around an arbor in a way that looks natural."

Writer: "So we should not try to succeed at wabi sabi writing?"

Basho: "If you must write, if there is nothing else as important to you, then write. But your writing should grow like a living thing out of the soil of your life. By writing, you may create some wabi things and by writing you may show some sabi shades. It is a worthwhile goal, but it may take you many years and it may take you to many places."

Writer: "Will you come on this journey with us and share your wisdom about wabi sabi writing?"

Basho: "With friends the dusty road that is long and winding becomes a pathway to another country, an inner country where no road may go. There can be no better destination."

Each stage of Basho's own journey has important lessons on how to become a wabi sabi writer. Basho was always inspired by nature, writing, and art, and he took advantage of his samurai heritage to gain a solid education in the classics. He immersed himself in the beauty he would later call wabi sabi and realized that his chosen form of expression, writing, could not only convey the beauty he saw but could also be an avenue of enlightenment. The remainder of this book is laid out on the bones of his life.

By practicing his art with a community of like-minded people, he sifted out the most important elements and taught them to others who came to him, or invited him to come to them, because his mastery was legendary. The four chapters that follow this one are about being a wabi sabi writer, focusing on the effect wabi sabi has on who you are. They reflect the formation of Basho as a person. The four chapters after that reflect how Basho applied wabi sabi to the act of writing itself. Each chapter in the first part of this book mirrors another chapter in the second part so that each state of being is reflected in an act of doing. Inspiration is reflected in motivation, education is reflected in community, and so on. To begin our journey down Basho's road we will look at inspiration, that marvelous and bewildering phenomenon that sparks our desire to write. Put on your grass sandals and paper coat. The road calls us on.

Summary

1. A wabi sabi writer reminds readers about a beauty they have forgotten.

2. Your writing will never be perfect or finished or lasting, but wabi sabi can make it authentic and memorable.

3. Wabi sabi is a way of living that is unusually conducive to writing.

4. Basho can teach us how to write from a deep and intuitive familiarity with wabi sabi beauty.

Two

Inspiration:
to make an impression,
write with your feet

ALPINE MEADOW

WE TRY TO FIND NAMES

FOR THE COLORS

Writer: "Basho, what inspired you?"

Basho: "Great books, fellow writers, and inspirational places. When I was a young man I attended Renga sessions, where a master poet would start us off with an inspired verse, and we would join in the creation of a long linked verse poem. It was exciting and challenging. When I became a Master Poet, groups from all over the country invited me to come and teach them and I went because it meant that along the way I could visit places where great poems had been written. I noticed what was the same and what had changed in the decades or centuries since the classic poems had been written. I found a new awareness of the transience of things and was stirred to write about it."

Writer: "Was that a satisfying process?"

Basho: "So satisfying that I became restless when I was back home again. I couldn't wait to get out to the places that inspired me."

Writer: "Why do your accounts of those journeys barely mention the time you spent in Renga sessions? Was the travel more inspiring?"

Basho: "The poems I wrote with my students and friends were published and enjoyed for many years, but I wanted to also write about that private experience. I wrote the travel journals from solitary inspiration, wabi inspiration. Those journals are not just diaries of stops on my teaching circuit. To just write about visiting this friend, this student, that famous shrine, and so on, well there is little poetry in that. There is more poetry in missing a friend than in meeting him. On one occasion I wrote: 'You weren't home when I came. Even the plum blossoms were in another yard.'"

Writer: "Should writers seek out the famous spots you did?"

Basho: "I didn't write so that others would go to the places I went. I wrote so that they would want to travel into poetry itself. You don't need to know *where* to go; you need to know how to go. I used to tell my students, 'do not simply follow the footsteps of famous writers; seek what they sought.'"

Writer: "What did they seek?"

Basho: "They sought what was eternal in the things that were transitory."

Writer: "Aren't those opposites?"

Basho: "When you see clearly into a fleeting moment, you glimpse eternity."

Inspiration Strikes

Inspiration is the pearly sediment of experience. In your busy day, thousands and thousands of impressions and perceptions sluice through the miner's box in your brain, and only a very few cast off anything heavy enough to collect as poetic memory. Those few silvery drops of rarefied existence form the core of your writing. You gather words around them. You re-create the sound of dry leaves crinkling in a fire, the color of cats' fur where it has just been licked, the smell of burning tires. And after you connect those sensations to characters or topics, your writing will terrify you with its beauty. When you have a fervor as strong as greed to translate your rarefied experiences into words, to communicate them before the flame of your attention wavers and you slip off the beam of light and into the dark slowness of forgetting, that is inspiration.

The High Way

It is Saturday morning. Adults are asleep or idling over coffee and the paper, and in their weekend slippers they have given up the street to children. Noisy, raucous, silly, teasing, blistered, tearful, laughing, excited like starlings at suet; their high polystyrene exchanges ricochet through my open window. Parents sometimes forget to listen, on purpose, and, just like subatomic particles, the innocence of children exists only when someone is looking or listening. The rest of the time kids muscle their way into life to explore politics and war firsthand. This morning, amid the juvenile chaos, amid the patterns forming within their language, comes a clear and common word: storm. The word penetrates the stream of their babble, and I go to the window and look up. There, rolling down the island, above the trees, scraping the tops of the mountains, a storm dark and heavy. I watch its shadow move along the side of Mount Benson, followed by a curtain of mist and rain. In a minute it is upon us, drawing quick upturned faces before little bodies bolt for cover. This storm is clearing the air of dust and anger and children. Small bodies all along the street head into houses.

Past me my own offspring clamor, "I get the computer!" "Do not, it's my turn." "Da-ad, he had it already this morning." "What," I stammer, ". . . what about that video we rented?" "Okay, but afterwards *I* get the computer." "Okay." And in a few minutes, the artificial sounds of voices and explosions and competing soundtracks.

In the time until the movie ends, I do what I long to do—lace up my boots, grab my hat and raincoat, and enter the downpour. This rain that rolls off the roofs all down the street reclaims me for silence—a paradoxical silence of water sound and thunder. I walk past houses and see, through their windows, children drying their hair, pulling off shirts; I see parents blinking and glancing out at the lightning. Turning away, they retreat with their children to dryness, to electronic noise.

This Saturday-morning-storm-created wilderness, a lonely expanse that moments ago was clogged with games and noise, takes on a new role. Now, only water careens along the knobbly surface into the slots of storm sewer grates. I wander a transformed ribbon of inspiration and reach the park before the rain ends. I slip soundlessly between the leaves and idle there amidst the drips, waiting for lightning to strike, waiting for inspiration.

Basho's Journey

The trips that Basho took by foot were more than casual walks on a Saturday morning; he faced long journeys over thousands of miles with very real dangers along the way, mostly from the physical hardships of travel and exposure to the harsh weather, but also from bandits and robbers. That Basho could travel in this way at all was testament to the foresight of the political leaders in power at the time. The military destruction of the Toyotomi clan in 1615 marked a profound change in Japanese history. With all rivals silenced or killed, the new Shogunate enacted sweeping changes across the country. Christianity had been banned a year earlier, and by 1635 the government had forbidden all travel overseas. Because of this ban, people like Basho traveled deeper into their own country.

It was also the start of the *sankin kotai* system, which required *daimyo* (local political leaders) to reside one year in their home province and one year in Edo (present-day Tokyo). Consequently, the leaders traveled at least once a year from their homes to Edo and back again. This sudden increase in the movement of officials and the need for safe trade among cities prompted a national road improvement and construction project. With the movement of people and the relaxation of class barriers, other things began to flow down these roads. Ideas, arts, crafts, and books made their way even into the rural areas. Literacy was officially encouraged, and in 1639 all foreign books were banned to encourage the reading and writing of Japanese. Most ports were closed to foreign ships. It was the start of *sakoku*, a period of cultural isolation. In a way it was a wabi time, a time of solitude and introspection. Sometimes isolation is a good thing, especially when it promotes reading, writing, and the exploration of what it means to be Japanese, or what it means to be you.

Three years after Japan was shut off from the world, Basho was born. His father was a low-ranking samurai, and when Basho was old enough he was apprenticed into the service of Todo Yoshitado, a relative of the daimyo who ruled the province where Basho lived. Basho served in a capacity similar to a page, but his master was only two years older than he was. The two became good friends, studied together, played together, and found interests that they both enjoyed, including writing verse. They were together all through their teens, and Basho might have gone on to live a privileged life writing courtly verse for the amusement and enjoyment of his friends if it had not been for the sudden death of his master and friend when Basho was only twenty-two. Rather than stay on with the family of his dead master, Basho traveled to Kyoto to pursue his passion for writing and explore the many business opportunities that had become available in the new era of stability and prosperity. Kyoto was the cultural capital of Japan at that time and had a powerful effect on the young man. He had already published numerous poems; a year later, when he was twenty-three, another thirty-one of his poems were published in a popular anthology. Most of these poems were written in the style of the day during Renga sessions. Basho considered poetry to be an important dialogue between poets, whereby a great aesthetic achievement was made together that could not be made separately. The resulting linked verses were like elaborate songs with interwoven melodies, extended and built upon by each poet who participated. It is clear that at this stage in his life the classical themes and the ethos of the literary community were the primary inspirations for his work.

Here is one of the Renga that Basho coauthored:

GIVEN THEIR FREEDOM
THE PET QUAIL—EVEN THE TRACKS
HAVE DISAPPEARED—SODAN

RICE SHOOTS LENGTHEN
IN A SOFT BREEZE—CHINSEKI

A CONVERT
STARTS BY GOING OVER
SUZUKA PASS—BASHO

In this poem, Sodan's evocative first verse, or hokku, is followed by Chinseki's link, which contrasts the absent quail with the growth of the rice in the field, then cleverly alludes to an older poem that speaks of the cries of quail in a breeze. Basho picks up the tender image of the new rice shoots and echoes their freshness with that of a youth heading off to a monastery. The image we are left with is one of quail and a young person leaving the rice fields behind, and experiencing the hardships but also the freedoms of leaving home. There are deep questions evoked by this poem. Are the quail and the convert really freer away from the farm? Is the spiritual path one that frees or binds a person?

Imagine what it was like to be part of a gathering where such exercises in poetic spontaneity were practiced. In a way, you are part of a similar process that is going on now on a grand scale. Literature builds literate people who take inspiration from what they read and echo back strains of other authors' beauty in their own writing. In this way, we have an ongoing song woven of books and thoughts and ideas that resonate with chords of insights, like a great opus of language rising to crescendos, subsiding into harmonies, and pulsing onward with the bright sound of synergy.

When Basho was recognized as a Master Poet himself, he was in great demand to judge poetry competitions and lead Renga sessions. He wrote commentary and edited books. At the age of thirty-seven, still enjoying the stimulation of the artistic community in Edo, Basho was presented with a small house from his students in appreciation of his teaching. It was in front of this house that a banana tree was planted as a gift. The teacher identified with the humble plant. It had sensitive leaves that tore in strong wind, it had small inauspicious flowers, and it made nice rustling sounds in the wind. In Japanese this plant is called *basho*. Until this time, the Master Poet (who had been born Matsuo Kinsaku) had written under various pen names, but now, in this plant, he found himself. Perhaps because of his own identification with the plant, or because others identified him as the teacher from the banana hut, or for both reasons, he became known simply as Basho. It was while living at this home that he wrote his famous crow poem:

ON A WITHERED BRANCH
A CROW SETTLES
AUTUMN EVENING

This poem, with its single image of a dark bird descending on a dead branch, captures the feeling both of night descending and of autumn approaching its end. The sabi of the poem is strong. It was a turning point in Basho's writing.

The shift away from humorous verse to poems with emotional resonance reflects his growing sensitivity to mature themes and might have been inspired by his life experiences. The banana hut burned down after only a year, and in the same year Basho received news that his mother had died. The shift in his writing may also have had something to do with his study of Zen. He had been writing three-line hokku by themselves for some time in a form we would later know as haiku. The desire to say more with less and to live an idealized life of simplicity and creativity infused his writing. In *Shriveled Chestnuts*, an anthology of poems Basho and his disciples published the year after the fire, there is a noticeable lack of crude and vulgar themes. The book focuses on tender ordinary moments of profound insight.

That winter, when Basho returned from a stay in Kai Province, his friends and disciples presented him with a new basho hut, but the attention and admiration of his students could not make up for the loneliness he felt now that both his parents were dead and he was facing midlife as a bachelor. We know that Basho had at some point prior to this learned of the Yamabushi, mountain ascetics who practiced extremely demanding disciplines that included standing in cold mountain waterfalls and walking on coals. Basho was attracted to the rigor, dedication, and stamina of these monks and identified with the seriousness of their character.

Pilgrimage to Poetry

Walking is a series of controlled falls. Each step forward shifts our center of gravity. In harmony with this fall, our bodies extend a leg to catch the center and balance it momentarily before it is cast forward again. We can do this with our writing—throw ourselves off balance in order to catch our balance again as we move forward.

When I first read Basho's travelogues, I had the sense that he was pleased to recklessly abandon himself to the dangers of the road and the bitterness of the elements. The title of his first major travelogue illustrates this point. It is called "Travelogue of a Weather Beaten Skeleton," and refers to the condition he was in at the end of the trip. In fact, the first haiku in the account puts it directly:

RESIGNED TO BE

A WEATHERED SKELETON

WIND PIERCES BODY AND MIND

After some study, I discovered that this embrace of hardship and pain had connections to a spiritual tradition Basho admired. The act of touring the country to visit important sites has the earmarks of a religious pilgrimage. One of the most well known of these pilgrimages was first done by Soo, a monk in the Tendai school of Buddhism. Born in 831, Soo took on legendary status when the god of perseverance appeared to him in a waterfall, saying, "All the peaks on this mountain are sacred. Make pilgrimages to its holy places following the instructions of the spirits of the peaks." Soo believed in a type of practice in which every stone and blade of grass was worthy of respect and able to communicate something important about the spiritual path. Soo took this instruction to heart and spent a great deal of time wandering in wild places. There had long been a role for such wanderers in Japan, and after Soo's death the practice was expanded by enthusiastic students, including some of the royal family. The wandering became ritualized into regular pilgrimages to various holy sites in remote mountainous locations, and the requirements of these pilgrimages became more and more arduous as more people sought to follow the routes. Eventually, the requirements became so arduous that most people lost interest. Basho took the idea of the wandering ascetic and applied the practice to a set of important literary locations. In doing this, he struck upon important elements that passed like memes from one generation to the next. Here are four of them:

1. Wandering is essential for writers.

2. Have a rough itinerary but take side trips. Basho taught that insight came in flashes when a writer was idly doing something unplanned. You have to set out with a goal in mind but be ready at a moment's notice to drop the goal so that you can attend to the insight.

3. Austerity and hardship are important. They tune the senses and make the travel more heroic. The underdog and the antihero had great significance to the literary world of medieval Japan, and Basho had no qualms about casting himself in that role.

4. A beautiful location can foster a receptive state of mind. Gazing upon the vastness of the cosmos, the power of a raging sea, or the terrifying beauty of a storm are ways to open perception wide. Awe and wonder are great triggers for the creative impulses.

Perhaps my sojourn into the rain on this Saturday morning does not quite live up to the demanding ideal of the wandering mendicant seeking inspiration through austerity and hardship, but I believe any degree of deliberate journeying accomplishes the same goal, if to a lesser degree. The fact of the matter is that Basho was not a zealot or a masochist. His routes were based around invitations he received to teach and lead Renga sessions all over the country. This was how he made his living. The edict that encouraged literacy in all the classes, including the merchants and farmers, resulted in a large group of people who found they liked reading and writing and wanted to learn more. Basho and the other samurai-turned-teachers were in demand. Imitating the pilgrims and mountain ascetics was good for inspiration, good for his reputation, and good for business.

Space, Place, Nature

Thomas Heyd of the Department of Philosophy at the University of Victoria writes about Basho's wandering, "The act of leisurely, albeit attentive, traversing (of) the land in a relatively unaided way—has an aesthetic that may help us to recover a sense of the depth of space, of the real diversity of places, and of our human lives within the larger context of nature."

Warren Hamilton Lewis, the brother of C. S. Lewis, recorded his own travelogue of a walking trip he and his brother took up the Wye Valley in Wales in the winter of 1934. The similarities between the Lewis brothers' trip and Basho's journeys are striking. Both Warren and Basho describe with engaging clarity their travels through beautiful countryside, the interesting people they met, and the deep and satisfying conversations they had along the way. Warren described each day with its trials and pleasures and summarized the trip with this telling comment: "Its only real fault is that it has given me aesthetic indigestion: I am not constituted to absorb beauty in such very large helpings."

See the Scenery

While sitting on the stone wall of a rest stop overlooking a deep valley in the Rocky Mountains, I looked up to see a large bus pull into the small parking lot. The doors opened and thirty-six tourists filed out. They approached the wall upon which I was sitting, pointed their cameras out over the expanse of landscape, snapped off a few shots, and filed back onto the bus, which drove away within minutes. At the time it happened, I judged these folks for their lack of true appreciation of the beauty they were looking at. Years later, while studying Basho, I remembered those tourists and wondered why people travel. The tourists I saw that day only had time to stop and take a quick photo. They didn't have time to be present at a place because there were other places they wanted to see. When they were back home, would they have time to reflect on their trip, would they remember the subtle lighting, the smell in the air, the people they met? Or would their photographs be mere trophies to impress family and friends? "Look where I was, look what I saw." My judging turned to sorrow. These people could have had so much more than a bus tour. Here are eight tips to ensure that your next trip is more than a gathering of photos:

1. Decide ahead of time that you will take your awareness with you and be where you are.

2. Take a friend who is looking for the same experience. Basho usually traveled with a fellow writer, and along the way they talked about books, writing, and art.

3. Travel slowly and make contact with the environment and weather. C. S. Lewis insisted on walking; Jack Kerouac hitchhiked. Others have gone by bicycle or horseback, kayak or canoe or sailboat. The most important thing is to slow down and not be in a hurry.

4. Do your homework ahead of time. Basho knew places by the poems that had been written there. His main motivation was to stand where other writers had stood and see what they saw. Places with historical significance can trigger curiosity about the characters involved and the events that made history.

5. Practice mindfulness. Notice the flowers, the animals, the buildings, the people, the landscape. Feel the rain, smell the soil, eat the local food. Listen to people's voices, their way of speaking, and the phrases they use. Be a sponge; soak in the ethos of a place.

6. Make notes. The more you write, the more you will have to write about. Something about the discipline of writing will start your creative juices flowing. If all you can write is descriptions of your surroundings, do that, but be open to deeper themes. Sometimes in places that are out of the ordinary you will encounter things that will trigger emotions and insights you would not have any other way. These are gifts that you need to accept and integrate into your life. Let everything that is inside

flow onto the page, and look for the details that have triggered your intense feelings. If they did it for you, chances are they will do it for your readers. Look for haiku moments and write them down, even if you don't have the right words or phrases at the time.

7. Take a picture. Not like the tourists; take wabi sabi shots. Photograph what is authentic or different, what will remind you of the place when you are back home. Look for wabi sabi faces. If you are brave enough, ask those people if you can take their pictures. Tell them you are a writer and that their faces inspire you. Ask them to tell you their story. Look at those pictures when you get home and try to tell their story, even if you don't know it. Make it up—that's what you do.

8. Go through your notes and look for common threads. If you have faithfully recorded the images that inspired you, the thoughts you had, and your feelings about the places, there will be patterns you can build on. As you listen to Basho's advice, you may discover a way past vacation to vocation.

Listening to the Masters

Vincent van Gogh wrote, "Many people do not copy, many others do—I started on it accidentally, and I find that it teaches me things, and above all it sometimes gives me consolation. And then my brush goes between my fingers as a bow would on the violin, and absolutely for my own pleasure." Here, Van Gogh describes the curious fact that beautiful art inspires us to create our own beauty. I have found this to be true with audio books. Getting together for Renga sessions in the way that Basho did is not as easy for us as it was for Basho. We are simply too busy. Writing groups, which serve a similar purpose, are hard to maintain over time.

I started listening to audio books when we had small children in the house and I had less time to sit and read. With an audio book I could prepare a meal, change a diaper, or clean a floor while the author or narrator read to me. In fact, the presence of that narrative thread during these tasks made them easier to face. But something else happened as well. I found that sometimes the power and richness of a work would trigger an overwhelming desire to write and I would wash and dry my hands and reach for the pen. Over the years, I have gone back to some favorite audio books again and again because they continue to inspire and motivate me. You may prefer to read books, but something about the audio format seems closer to Basho's recommendation to write within a community. Here is a highly subjective list of contemporary audio books that I believe will inspire you with their deep wabi sabi qualities.

Summer Gone written by David Macfarlane, read by Eric Schneider. Macfarlane captures the essence of summer, summer camp, and a camp leader who instills the love of nature in campers through his own quiet convictions. The main character is an ordinary man who struggles with the consequences of his sensitivity and sensuality. Details paint the text full of sunlight, and you swear the pages are made of dry grass.

Fugitive Pieces written by Anne Michaels, narrated by Neil Munro and Diego Matamoros. It is impossible to categorize this poetic masterpiece, but it is filled with wabi sabi images of loss, life, and literature. Each time I listen to it I am impressed with its economy and precision—not one word is wasted or superfluous. To achieve this level of poetic power primarily through the juxtaposition of clear and detailed descriptions is remarkable.

Unless written by Carol Shields, read by Joan Allen. A story about integrating the past into the present, *Unless* is one of Shields's most complex books. Yet it seems a simple narrative about an ordinary family. That ordinariness unfolds in a rich tapestry of family attachments. When I listen to it I find myself thinking deeply about my own domestic life. Strong and honest and full of curious observations and insights, the integrity of the tale moves the reader from angst to acceptance.

The Shipping News written by E. Annie Proulx, read by Robert Joy. Proulx's voice shines from this book with aching emotional purity. Character development is the key to this novel's wabi sabi attractions. Each character is defined by convincing turns of phrase, gestures, and actions. Joy's accents and voices are enjoyable and add to the feel of the book.

For the Time Being written by Annie Dillard, read by David Birney. I considered listing Dillard's *Pilgrim at Tinker Creek* because it has such a Walden-esque feel, but the audio book of hers I go back to again and again is this one, perhaps because of Birney's subtle and rich narration. This is not only a deeply wabi sabi book that explores hard questions about nature and deformity, but it is also masterfully composed, using multiple threads and themes woven together to produce moments of profound insight.

Quite a Year for Plums written and read by Bailey White. Odd yet lovable characters populate this book from cover to cover, and the pleasure of getting to know and understand them is satisfying. This is another carefully crafted book that presents only those events and details that matter, but presents them in warm tones and sharp relief. White's narration strikes me as both comfortingly familiar and pleasingly unusual, like a visit to an eccentric aunt's house to hear the news about town.

A River Runs Through It written by Norman Maclean, read by Ivan Doig. Poetic turns of phrase complement this portrait of the lives of two brothers and fill this book with a sort of mystery, as if some deep current of lyrical vulnerability flows beneath its pages.

The Curious Incident of the Dog in the Night-Time written by Mark Haddon, read by Jeff Woodman. The style of this book is hard to describe. It is told in the first person from inside the mind of a boy with Asperger's syndrome, who is writing a book for school. We see the world in vivid detail and as if from a slightly more intense perspective. The "normal" people in the boy's life are stripped to their personas from his almost clinical perspective. Emotional life is revealed as curious and irrational, and humorous.

Zen and the Art of Motorcycle Maintenance written by Robert M. Pirsig, read by Michael Kramer. A father and son travel the back roads of America while coming to terms with their mental illness. The journey motif allows for an extended and interesting exploration of philosophical questions resulting in bright sharp insights when related to the developing themes in the book. The "voice" of this writer is measured and precise, just as I imagine a mechanic's would be.

The Intimate Merton: His Life from His Journals edited by Jonathan Montaldo, read by Patrick Hart. Editor Jonathan Montaldo has chosen those sections of Thomas Merton's extensive journals that reveal the human, and wabi sabi, side of Merton. Merton has always been a favorite of mine, and this collection shows his inner passions and poetic genius.

Three

Education:
find your voice by moonlight

Writer: "Basho, what kind of education should a writer have?"

Basho: "Learn the rules and techniques for good writing from teachers who have read and loved the classics. Then explore *furyu*."

Writer: "What is furyu?"

Basho: "Furyu means 'wind and stream' or 'in the way of the wind and stream.' It is a way of living that gradually expands your sense of beauty, taste, and aesthetic appreciation."

Writer: "Where did the idea of furyu come from?"

Basho: "The Japanese word *furyu* evolved from the Chinese word *fengliu*. Originally, the Chinese word was used to express the unpredictability of human existence; human existence was 'wind and stream.' The first Japanese writers thought it described their own aesthetic sensibility. It was applied to art that reflected the fleeting beauty of daily life. Since capturing such beauty has always been a challenge, great writers made it their highest ideal. Those who wished to flatter writers used 'furyu' as a compliment, and soon people used it to refer to any well-crafted piece of art, many of them far removed from flow and change. That happens with a word, but then the original Chinese definition became popular again, but with a slight twist. It was now used to describe *transcendence* from daily life. The

Buddhists taught that this transcendence occurred on a religious path, but the Taoists taught that it was the elegance of nature that lifted a person out of despondency and resignation. The tea masters preferred the Taoist meaning and used furyu in combination with *suki* (the devotion to an art) to naturalize their practice and find transcendence through harmony with nature."

Writer: "And you sought the same transcendence through writing?"

Basho: "People believed that a writer had to retire from society in order to achieve a certain elegance of literature, what they called *fuga*. The two terms became almost formulaic: furyu leads to fuga. A writer removes herself to a natural setting and meditates on her surroundings and produces beautiful writing that helps her readers transcend the ordinary. Only the most superb writing really does this. As a young man this seemed to me to be a worthy goal."

Writer: "And did you achieve it?"

Basho: "My experience with the life of seclusion showed me that it was not retirement that fostered furyu, but something else. That 'something else' was hinted at in the Chinese poetry and Taoist writings I read. I wanted to write like the Taoist sages, who seemed to grasp some elemental beauty beyond words. They weren't just criticizing Confucius and his artless systems; they were pointing to a way beyond formulas. This was liberating and I wanted that freedom. But I have to tell you that this kind of freedom, though it allows you a tremendous openness to change, goes beyond what you can learn in a school."

Writer: "How does a person learn it then?"

Basho: "It isn't really something you learn as much as something you decide to do. It is the choice to stay open, to point your boat into the fast water rather than hit the rocks."

Writer: "What are the rocks?"

Basho: "Fear is the greatest obstacle, the fear of nature's dangers, but also fear of loss or of not getting what you want. But there are other rocks. Cleverness is one. If a writer's own cleverness is too obvious it spoils the flow; you run into the stones of cleverness like a boat runs into boulders in rapids. When I say cleverness I am primarily referring to sarcastic wit that is really a way of saying, 'Look how clever I am.' A writer who carefully observes the stream of existence will not have to resort to cleverness; will chart a course that steers very close to it but slips past cleverness without touching it. Readers and writers both get hung up on cleverness. I should know. I was infatuated with clever poems and wrote many myself. But I finally realized that as distracting as the stones in a river are, you don't want to get stranded on them. When I talk of slipping past cleverness I'm not talking about avoiding the rapids altogether; that is avoiding cleverness for the calm pools of dullness. No, I insist on the rapids. That is where your education lies, that is where you find wabi sabi."

What the Samurai Knew

One night on the outskirts of a town in Japan, a burglar made his way through the dark streets looking for his next easy target. He spotted a small well-kept house that showed no lamplight and was completely dark inside. For several minutes, he stood motionless outside the house listening, and he heard no sounds at all from inside. He drew his sword and quietly entered the house to see what he might steal.

"You are making too much noise," a voice called out. "My money is in a silk purse under the tatami mat."

Startled, the thief slashed his sword in front of him and strained to see in the dark house where only the dim light of stars showed through an open window. On a cushion in an adjacent room, he finally made out a motionless shape that he took to be a man sitting in meditation. The thief did not know that this was the home of Shichiri Kojun, a samurai who had practiced meditation and martial arts for fifty years. The thief found the purse where Shichiri said it was and dumped the coins into his hand.

"Don't take it all. I have to pay my bills tomorrow," Shichiri called out from the other room, "and ask politely when you want something."

"May I have some money?" the thief said into the darkness, surprised by his own response.

"Yes," Shichiri replied.

The thief put half of the coins back into the purse and replaced it under the tatami mat.

"Thank a person when he gives you a gift," Shichiri called out.

"Thank you," the thief said in a soft voice, bowed toward the motionless figure, and ran from the house.

Later that night, the thief was caught breaking into another house and the authorities carted him off to jail, returned the stolen items to their rightful owners, and collected statements to use against the thief. When they came to Shichiri's house the samurai calmly listened as they explained that the thief had been seen running from his house. "Some of this money must be yours," they said, and Shichiri looked down at the shiny coins they held out.

"The man you speak of did come into my house this evening but he did not steal my money, he politely asked for it and I gave it to him. I asked him to leave enough to pay my bills and he did. Then he thanked me politely and left." Shichiri showed the authorities his silk purse and they saw that it still contained a number of coins. "Clearly the man was poorer than I am. I wish I could have given him something more. I wish I could have given him an appreciation for the beauty of the moon." Shichiri motioned toward the sky, where the full moon was rising into view. "Give the coins that were mine back to the man you say is a thief, they are his now."

Years later, when the thief was released from prison, he returned to Shichiri's house and stood outside watching the elderly samurai practicing his exercises as he had for more than sixty years. When Shichiri finished he looked out at the man and said, "I see you want to learn how to appreciate the beauty of the moon."

The man bowed politely and said, "Your generosity confounded me, your instruction corrected me, and your invitation intrigues me. Can an old thief like me give up coins for the moon?"

"When you learn to appreciate the beauty of the moon," Shichiri said, "the glimmer of coins will lose its appeal."

The burglar studied devotedly with Shichiri until his master died several years later. In that time he learned to appreciate the beauty of the moon. The former thief received furyu from his master; he learned to appreciate not just the beauty of the moon, but to look for beauty everywhere, even in unlikely places.

This former thief returned to the man who he knew could teach him how to desire something other than money. The freedom from the desire for money is only possible when the value of other things is made clear. That is one of the main goals to keep in mind as you pursue your education. Rather than seeing your education as a path to a high standard of living, see your education as instruction on how to live.

Voice

What did the thief find to replace his longing for money? By choosing to stay open, to appreciate the elegance of nature, to be at home with change and impermanence, he found that his desires could be examined and considered. Many people appreciate a beautiful sunset, or a lovely vista, but few choose to have more of this natural beauty and less money. We grow comfortable with the conveniences of a moneyed life. The samurai's balance of enough money to pay his bills and the freedom to give away the rest was possible because he had decided to live a certain kind of life free from certain constraints. He had fashioned a life of beauty that held near its summit the desire to share that appreciation of beauty with others.

The story of Shichiri is a salvation story. The old samurai offered the thief a way out of his self-destructive and limiting lifestyle. When you choose values such as these, when you choose to follow a path that leads to furyu and ultimately to wabi sabi, then you will find that it changes who you are, which changes your voice. Can you hear in the details of this story the character and wisdom of the old samurai?

Let me illustrate this point with a story of how a value shaped my own voice. During my thirteenth summer I grew three inches and my voice broke and then dropped. The year before that a teacher, exasperated with my emotional outbursts in class, shouted at me, "Be quiet, you sound like an old woman!"

The Choice

I stand in the stationery store with my mother picking out school supplies for the September term. I turn around to see a classmate I haven't seen all summer looking at me from head to toe. His eyes travel up and down my body and his mouth hangs open.

"Hi Carl," I say.

"Man, have you ever grown!" is all he can stammer.

That year I learned firsthand about male power, learned that being bigger meant you could intimidate kids like Carl, that having a deeper voice meant you could drown out girls and other people with softer voices. One day, while I was intimidating Carl behind the school, a childhood friend said, "Leave him alone, he's okay, what'd he ever do to you? I thought you were his friend." My face flushed and I looked into Carl's eyes. I had always been the kid bullies picked on; now I was being the bully. It was a pivotal moment, there on the Trafalgar school ground, one of those moments that are depicted in movies by swinging the camera around and around the actor to indicate both disorientation and the intensity of the moment. I sat on the curb embarrassed and ashamed, swallowing hard. I never did it again; those few words from my boyhood pal who knew me when I was the victim jolted me into myself and allowed me to see Carl again, see him as a person I liked and did not want to hurt.

Male stereotypes pull hard at a boy; male society encourages a kind of brutish toughness. But my heart was born tender and gentle; my strength increased when I turned away from male pride. I refused to become like the bullies who competed for positions of status in circles of power by hurting others. This was a difficult stand to take, and I stretched out across my limited experience for something to support my new conviction. What I found were the gospels.

During confirmation classes at St. Andrew's-by-the-Lake, I had glimpsed an odd kind of man who was both attractive and frightening. Jesus, strong and nonretaliatory, tolerant of outcasts and misfits, and intolerant of bullies and self-righteous egotists, seemed like the kind of radical I wanted to be. I joined a group of kids who met at a local church on Friday nights. I didn't know at the time that this decision would affect my inner voice. I didn't realize that choices alter your mental vocal cords, but I found something important inside myself, and it didn't matter if it was at odds with the rules of male culture.

I didn't entirely give up insults and clever remarks, but the voice that was inside me, the voice that was humming with a new tension, began to feel like something worth having. I became evangelical about alternatives to stereotypes. I started writing poems about gender issues. It was a floundering beginning full of private passion and fear, but it was a beginning. I had no idea how long it would take to develop my writer's voice, but just as my physical larynx had changed over a summer, my literary larynx had changed with a sudden growth in values.

Something to Say

William Brodrick said on the publication of his successful novel *The 6th Lamentation*, "I'm not sure there is a secret (to my success), and 'success' is one of those problematic words. I waited until I knew what I wanted to write about, and how; then I made it the defining goal of my life—which was almost certainly a dangerous thing to do."

I applaud Brodrick's courage to wait until he knew what he wanted to write about, and how, and make that the defining goal of his life. It sounds simple, but it contains a very difficult word, "waited." It seems strange for a book about writing to encourage you to wait, but what you are waiting for is not some fully formed image that will drive you on to completion; you are waiting for your voice to clear. You are waiting for the ghost of Basho's frog to be cast out of your own throat and croak about in your writing. This cleared frog will produce a lot of words as you explore the subjects and ideas that matter to you. Don't settle for the ghost of Basho's frog, however; it is not "The Thing" you will write about. It is just a representative sent on ahead, a scout looking for the promised land.

While you are searching for that one defining goal of your career or while you are facing a subject that seems too large to get words all the way around, do what Basho did. Read, study, investigate, and keep writing. Basho spent his teens and early twenties reading the classics, studying under various teachers, and writing for fun with his master and friends. This is what a good education is, an opportunity to immerse yourself in fine writing and fine instruction, to study various subjects under various teachers, and always to write and write and write.

William Brodrick waited until he knew what he wanted to write about, then he sat down to write his first book. Perhaps that's another way of saying he waited until he found his voice, until the patterns in his head were strong enough to produce an expression in words that would go beyond croaks and splashes. You will find that your voice will break out from time to time, and when you recognize it you will be on your road to that life-long passion Brodrick found, the passion of saying what you have to say, expressing words as if they were part of a stream flowing through you. You will begin to touch furyu.

Classics

In her book *Long Quiet Highway*, Natalie Goldberg says, "People would rather read about how to become a writer than read the actual products of writing: poems, novels, short stories." Is this a surprising quote to find in a book about writing? When I read Goldberg's book I thought back to my own beginnings as a writer. The truth is I was a writer before I was a reader. I made a few forays into the Trafalgar school library and liked the feeling of the place, but reading was difficult and the books I was given seldom grabbed my attention. I was a typical example of what Goldberg is talking about. I had a desire to express myself, but less desire to hear other people express themselves. Having a teacher like Goldberg might have helped.

When I remember my high-school English classes I feel waves of fear and failure wash over me. I cannot remember the books we studied or the discussions in class. Instead, I remember being distracted, uninterested, and also being laughed at for my shyness and inability to spell. The translations we read were stiff, and the teachers who stood at the front of the class were tired. They reserved their energy for the smart kids. I sat in class and dreamed of fishing, canoeing, swimming, hiking, and wandering stream banks and lakeshores. Early academic failure led to more academic failures, so by the time I reached junior high school I was relegated to remedial classes, where bullies and brawlers competed with the teachers for control of the classroom.

I gave up on English classes but continued writing poetry, inspired by songwriters such as Leonard Cohen and Bruce Cockburn. I grew to appreciate a diverse group of other lyricists, from Paul Simon to Mark Heard to Sam Phillips. These singers spoke in a language I could understand about subjects I related to. Shakespeare, Milton, and Dante remained locked in the ice of another world. I didn't know why we were supposed to read these authors and don't remember any teacher expressing his or her own personal love for them. These books may have been as beautiful as the moon, but all I saw was cold distant rock.

A friend of mine read contemporary poetry and showed me some of her favorites. The authors she liked wrote in a language I could understand but concentrated their attention on sex, drinking, money, and broken relationships. I was interested in nature, cosmology, theology, ethics, and changing the world. I wore a "no-nukes" button on my coat and visited a hippie holdout called the Preservation House with my long-haired friends. We drank coffee, talked about ideas, and gossiped about girls. Even the talk about girls was intellectual; a sort of romanticized storytelling involving idealized females. We were hungry for perfection, and this hunger eventually drew us to great books.

In *Long Quiet Highway*, Goldberg remembers her own education and comments on various teachers she had, the good and the bad. A teacher now herself, she emphasizes that reading literature can be hard, especially if you are young and don't understand the context, the idioms, and the concepts. A good teacher will help you understand why a great work of literature is great, point out revolutionary ideas, unique styles, unusual subjects, subtle tones, and hear the voice of each author.

I don't know if I would have appreciated a teacher like Goldberg when I was a teenager. I do know that for whatever reason, I didn't connect with one. After two years of college, however, I finally discovered a writing school that did have teachers who loved great books. I listened to them and they listened to me and encouraged me to keep croaking away at my voice. My work was painfully earnest and reflected my lack of awareness of literature. Fellow students would utter the names of authors I had never heard of, and I hoped no one would ask me what I thought of these literary giants. I was woefully unprepared, and my writing career took many years to develop. But perhaps that is exactly how it should have been.

When I was nineteen, writing painful self-centered and solipsistic pieces about my emotional dilemmas and naive ideas of God and the meaning of life, I had not been adequately exposed to models or mentors that I could emulate. In spite of this, those early college instructors understood my situation and knew I had something inside me that was worth the wait of years, even decades, before it would be ready for publication. They placed important books in my hands, challenged me to read, and forced me to produce writing week after week. Find such teachers if you haven't already; they can help in ways that reading alone cannot.

The Elegance of Nature

Basho begins his book *The Narrow Road to the Deep Interior* with these words, "The moon and the sun travel night and day. The years trail on without interruption. Whether steering a ship at sea or leading a horse on land, each person's life is a journey and the journey itself is home." In this opening passage, we have a wabi sabi philosophy for writers. Each person's journey is the place they belong. Journeying is our natural condition.

Basho observed that everything is in motion, and efforts to deny or ignore this are delusions. Rather than attempt to avoid this reality by establishing fixed defense points, fortresses, monuments, and statues, rather than relying on solid foundations, building stable homes from which to venture and return, Basho fixed himself to a different point of reference, a point caught up in the swirl of the storm. He synchronized his trajectory with the moving mass of patterns and codes, memes and ideas around him. With both emergence and acquiescence he was part of the dance. In this perpetual movement he attained stillness because he was moving relative to everything else.

In a river, a boat moves without effort if it is moving downstream. For Basho, travel was a home made of river with its foundation resting plumb on the shores of a lake. This home is surrounded by four sturdy walls: spring, summer, autumn, and winter. By sleeping on a walking horse Basho lost his need for control and so found direction.

This paradox of building a life on change scares me. It feels reckless, dangerous, and foolish. But what it does for a writer is create a sense of expectation, a sense that each moment may contain the experience that will open up something bracing and real, or something warm and meaningful, or something bright and sober, something worth sharing, something readers will not be able to put down.

This way of being is like carrying a hidden doorway in your pocket through which you can smuggle impressions, silent apprehensions, and private observations moment after moment because you are not expending effort to get anywhere. You can focus on the moment because each moment takes place inside your stillness, inside your own home. Being present in the motion, moment after moment, provides that secret chamber of awareness and gives a writer the chance to notice what is passing by before it is gone.

This presence of mind is what leads to insight, and once insight occurs it pulses through you into language. This is Basho's dialectical destination, his meandering city where each street harbors a poetic inn. This is living in the stream, writing from an ever-changing location, comfortable with being lost, satisfied with gifts instead of acquisitions. Writing from this location-free openness allows characters to leap from the watery impermanence of glimpses and sightings into a sort of half-life made up of narrative molecules decaying on the page, shooting their excess electrons into flesh and blood of readers who recognize in the writing their own faces.

We write to reveal, to learn, and to pass on our learning, and all of it comes from traveling at the speed of sight, breaking out of our sense that safety is anything but an illusion. The only real safety is to tell the journey well and rest in its incompletion. When it is done, when it is finished, you too will be done, and each coded message in your cellular residue will not tell as much about you as your smallest thought tamed and ridden from the wilderness onto the page.

Gary Snyder illuminates this in his book *The Practice of the Wild*. "It has always been part of basic human experience to live in a culture of wilderness," Snyder says. "There has been no wilderness without some kind of human presence for several hundred thousand years. Nature is not a place to visit, it is *home*—and within that home territory there are more familiar and less familiar places." Each one of us, from the time we are born until the time we die, moves through nature, what Snyder calls "the wilderness," and this movement itself is natural. We are made to wander, we are born to venture out, we trek the high ridges and deep valleys of existence; this is where we belong.

I remember a time, while hiking in the backcountry with my father, when we crossed over a ridge and gazed upon a great expanse of forest with no roads or blemishes. We looked out over Kokanee Glacier Provincial Park. On the map of British Columbia, the 32,035 hectares of Kokanee Glacier Park are a small green square among other green shapes blemishing the web of roadways with noticeable irregularity. Having seen it on the map and then seeing it stretched out in front of us made me realize how hard it is to imagine all the bear and deer and pikas and elk and fish and hummingbirds that are living in that bit of green on the map—not to mention humans puffing their way in and out of the alpine valleys. I realized that it was my job to tell that park to you, your job to tell me your park. And your park might be a traditional park with rustic signs made from logs. It might have park rangers who call you sir or ma'am. Or your park might be the place you park, the spot you go to that renews you and brings you back in touch with your wild side.

Some contemporary educators, questioning the effectiveness of institutional schooling, have suggested that we give each student a bit of land to manage; not to own, just to take care of. Being on a bit of land, even an abandoned city lot, has a profound influence on students, especially if part of their job is to observe and relate to the living systems there.

In her book *Little Men*, published in 1871, Louisa May Alcott described the Sunday afternoon ritual observed by Jo Bhaer and the students who live and learn at the Plumfield Estate School. The entire family would head out into the natural world; "Mr. Bhaer always went with them, and in his simple, fatherly way, found for his flock, 'Sermons in stones, books in the running brooks, and good in everything.'"

A recent caller on a radio talk show told of visiting classrooms to explain the Canadian gun registry to the children. He said he noticed a funny thing about kids these days. When he asked the children how many of them had been to Disneyland, about half the class would put up their hands. But when he asked how many of them had been to the top of the hill behind the school, only about four or five hands would go up. After seeing this trend repeated all over the province, he concluded that children are not going into nature like they used to, not exploring woods and meadows, partly, the caller was keen to point out, because parents are not taking them hunting and fishing and camping like they used to, but partly, I thought to myself, because Disneyland advertises.

This trend concerns me because it is dangerous to forget our connection to the real land, the land upon which grow all the wild things. As we become more suburban and sedentary as a culture, we forget about the source of the food we eat and the water we drink, and the beauty waiting there. Regardless of your view on guns and hunting, one thing that hunting does is bring people in contact with wilderness and the firsthand experience of killing an animal and eating it. Some people choose vegetarianism after such an experience. Others find that the experience is filled with complex and deep emotions, wild emotions, which do not respond easily to detached analysis. Instead of killing animals, other writers deliberately tend a garden, learning the wonder of eating a carrot pulled seconds before from the cool soil. Many writers procreate and raise children who are ambassadors to a cultured existence from the wildest possible realms.

We forget how much nature has to teach us because we turn away from our animal nature and focus on higher brain functions. Western culture has celebrated the successes of the cerebral cortex, posting for inspection a campus full of academic study based around rigorous standards that define what can be known, and how. Wabi sabi brings to the academic world a different sort of classroom; it brings the bumping childhood contact with the world, like Winnie the Pooh bumping down the stairs behind Christopher Robin. It brings stages and sages and burnt eyelashes from inspecting the fire for toasted marshmallows. Like an overstuffed station wagon returning from the lake, wabi sabi rattles along noticeable and memorable roads and lays dust against ancient trees. Remember it, notice it, write about it. Nature is everything.

Four

Wabi Sabi Beauty:

let poetry flow
from your attachments

BLOND GRASS

LIGHTS A SUMMER NIGHT

WITHOUT FIRE

Writer: "Why are wabi sabi things beautiful?"

Basho: "There is nothing you can see that is not a flower; there is nothing you can think that is not the moon."

Writer: "Excuse me?"

Basho: "My invitation to everyone interested in wabi sabi is to come out to view the truth of flowers blooming in poverty."

Writer: "What is it about flowers blooming in poverty that is so wabi sabi?"

Basho: "Confucius said, 'Everything has beauty, but not everyone sees it.' Wabi sabi is the kind of beauty people don't always see, like roadside flowers that are not as spectacular as a peony or a morning glory carefully planted in a private garden. The wild flowers contain something important that the cultivated flowers overdo. It is their uncultivated nature that makes them beautiful."

Writer: "Then we should focus on making our writing uncultivated?"

Basho: "Grasshoppers have wings as well as legs, yet we do not call them grassfliers."

Writer: "Grasshoppers spend most of their time hopping, so I guess that is why we call them grasshoppers."

Basho: "When people walk through a field of dry grass and grasshoppers scatter in front of them, they already have in their mind the word 'grasshopper,' and it automatically fills the linguistic slot for the insect they observe. It takes effort to see creatures without their names, to really look at these little beings as if they were a new species, never before observed. Look at the grasshopper in this way and you will find wabi sabi."

Writer: "A grasshopper is wabi sabi?"

Basho: "I learned to see wabi sabi from an old Buddhist sage named Saigyo. He said, 'As the nights grow cooler and autumn advances, the cry of the crickets grows weak and more distant.'"

Writer: "Ah, so the impermanence of crickets and grasshoppers is what is beautiful?"

Basho: "Impermanence isn't beautiful. But it makes the impermanent creature more beautiful."

Writer: "Isn't everything impermanent?"

Basho: "Yes, but we don't remember that. Even the moon will someday disappear, but for our short lives the moon seems eternal. The cricket, on the other hand, we witness his whole short life. Rikyu used to say, 'Each tea ceremony is the only tea ceremony.' I would say, 'Each cricket is the only cricket.'"

Writer: "Some have continued this idea and said that each poem is the only poem."

Basho: "Each moment is the only moment. It applies to everything."

Writer: "How does a writer convey this in a piece of writing?"

Basho: "If you are true to the moment and describe not just your feelings and impressions, but the details that inspired you, then your readers should be able to enter it as if it were the only moment. You can place yourself in a piece of writing, but you should only be part of the scene; you should not be trying to win a reader to your view of things."

Writer: "So you are talking about being objective?"

Basho: "No, I'm talking about being disciplined. Soin and his students used to talk about yugen in a poem, insisting that a good poem alludes to its real subject by referring to something else. Clouds and rain allude to sexual intimacy—that sort of thing. The trouble with this is that it becomes a sort of game. Spot the innuendo. Trying to say one thing and mean another can be fun and clever, but cleverness, you will remember, is a rock in the stream. Yugen may be a valid poetic quality, but metaphor isn't far behind."

Writer: "What's wrong with metaphor?"

Basho: "Metaphor is a poetic tool that can be used to good effect, but yugen has a deeper quality."

Writer: "How do you express yugen?"

Basho: "Soin relied on juxtaposition to hint at deeper meaning—putting two different images together to surprise us into beauty. Soin's group of followers, the Danrin or 'talkative forest,' succeeded in mastering this effect. I applauded them for moving away from the formalism and the tired rules of traditional poets but observed that they often ended up mired in wordplay and cleverness."

Writer: "What did you suggest instead?"

Basho: "It is good to avoid spelling out a subject too clearly and celebrating obvious beauty. It is easy to overdo poetic elements in writing. We all like it when writing opens up before us like a morning glory revealing its depth. Most of us would rather be shown something beautiful than be told that it is beautiful. You want a piece of writing to make you feel that you are coming upon the beauty on your own or seeing a beauty others have missed."

Writer: "You listed yugen as an important element in haiku. Did you mean the technique that Soin taught?"

Basho: "I was referring to the interplay of substance and form. The haiku that reveals seventy to eighty percent of its subject is good. The haiku that reveals fifty to sixty percent we never grow tired of. The part we see is the form; the part hidden is the substance. This is what poetry is all about, getting at the deep elegance. It is like a glimpse of a beautiful lake through some trees, hearing a bird song carried on the wind, smelling an herb's scent on your hands. These things are more beautiful because we are not observing them objectively. Since the time of the tea master Shuko we have understood that the moon obscured by clouds is more beautiful than a full moon on a clear night."

The Beauty of Being Awake

A college gymnasium on a cold November day hosts a basketball game between a group of local civic leaders and a visiting team of dwarves. The match is a fundraiser for the local Boys and Girls Club and I take my children to watch. This isn't something I would ordinarily do. For one thing I am not sure if this event is demeaning to dwarves, and for another I am a mediocre sports spectator, preferring to watch a horse graze or moonlight break into ribbons on a quiet bay. I wonder if I am supporting stereotypical portrayals of little people by attending this event. Is it just a sanitized version of the old carnival spectacle? And of less obvious concern, am I supporting artificial social constructs that encourage the division of citizens into winners and losers? I consider this dilemma, and look around at the people entering the gym. Spectators find their seats, parents chatter, children brag. There is an energy in the crowd as the game begins. After a few minutes, I realize that these people are not here to ogle at dwarves; they are here because the dwarves are playing basketball better than most people of average stature. The humor and antics still perpetuate the circus stereotype, but it is the skill and determination of these athletes that impresses everyone.

I brought my children to this event because I hoped they would see something in the event I was unable to, or find something in it I lost, or maybe they would lose something I hold too tightly. It is a hard thing to encourage your children to be someone you are not, to see something you have not. This is also true of writers and the characters they raise up with their words.

An old sage once told me, "All the people in your dreams at night are you, and all the characters you write about are too." Parenting and writing involve a struggle to let go of your self. When I first found wabi sabi, I realized that it was the beauty that would free my writing; a previously camouflaged mechanism at the back of the box that would allow me to slip out of myself and just write beauty into existence, just pick out those moments that I knew would speak beyond language. I like to imagine that if we were to wake up, in the way the Buddha did, we would see beauty in places we hadn't thought to look before. So I am here at this basketball game. My secret mission is to spy on the places I had not thought to look, to search for an opening, a hidden-in-plain-sight tab in the fabric of the place; a handle to open the liquid surface of time and allow a reader to slip into beauty with her whole body. Holistic pools at the hot spring of beauty, warmth soaking loose the crust of ugliness.

During halftime, sitting alone on the hard shiny bleachers while my children buy drinks at the concession window, I pull out Richard Wright's *Haiku: This Other World* and begin to read. This is one of my pools, a paper and print reservoir to wet my dry eyes and help me see. I am engrossed in the book when a woman takes the spot beside me and nudges my arm. "These little people are amazing, eh?"

"Yes," I agree, looking briefly at her and then out over the empty court.

"Good sports, too," she says. I consider how to respond to this comment. What does it mean to be a good sport? Usually it means to be a good loser, or lose gracefully. I think she means that despite their obvious handicap, they play the game valiantly. In this she is correct.

"Very good," I finally say.

"I hear they have certain physical conditions."

"You mean besides their short stature?"

"Yes, other problems, medical complications."

"I don't know," I respond, blinking as if to conjure up something helpful to say.

"What are you reading?" she asks. I show her the cover and she laughs.

"Reading haiku during a basketball game," she shakes her head. "That's a new one."

I smile and return to reading. I would rather read haiku, submerged in the pleasing waters of "this other world," than participate in small talk.

Wright's collection is one I have read more than once. I read and reread his poems not because they are consistently brilliant; I appreciate them in spite of the fact that he sticks doggedly to seventeen syllables and produces a series of poems in which sounds are given colors and colors are given sounds. Basho did it once effectively when he wrote:

SEA DARKENS
CALLS OF THE WILD DUCKS
GO FAINTLY WHITE

Poems by other poets using this same technique grow faintly transparent for me, but I give Wright some latitude because he was writing at a time when such "innovations" were first discovered in the West, and because when Wright gets it right it is sublime. He captures moments and conveys them so clearly that they evoke an emotion in me without any coercion or suggestion on his part. Consider this example:

A DEAD GREEN BEETLE
BOBBING ON A FLOWING CREEK,
BEATEN BY SPRING RAIN.

The alliteration of the sounds, the color of the beetle, the movement of the creek and the splashing of the rain on the creek surface give me a feeling of unsheltered wetness. Reading this poem, my hair feels wet. The sound of the rain and the smell of the creek bubble up in my imagination from these few lines. I see twigs and other debris amid the wavelets, imagine the moss-covered rocks along the shore, conjure a whole range of sensory experience all because of that bobbing bud-colored beetle.

Wright wrote a lengthy afterword for this book in which he presents information about the history of haiku and the aesthetics of the form. He focuses on the change of perception brought about by reading an effective haiku. What he applauds about the form is its quiet avoidance of intellectualism and emotionalism, focusing instead on nature in its best moments. Wright notes that Basho and his contemporaries were selective in the kind of nature they wrote about. They rarely wrote about natural disasters or about the brutal world of predation and survival of the fittest. When such elements are included in haiku of Basho's era they reflect an admiration for the perseverance and tenacity of living creatures that face the hardships of existence with a kind of stamina that is itself marbled with beauty. Perhaps this is what draws people to these events. It is the beauty of life, of overcoming challenges, of living life despite danger, pain, and loss; despite hardship, injury, bad luck.

The wabi man, which Basho continually held up as his model, is a man so in flow with nature that he sees his life as a series of haiku, each momentary poignancy surrounded by the void of whiteness that is both the paper upon which the haiku are written and the context within which life exists. The paper and the context is absence of form, or in a cool objective view—"death." This elemental and primal integration of life and death, of the moment and eternity, is the strumming, beating, bouncing beauty we call wabi sabi. As such, all of nature, moment after moment, plays out this beauty. Creatures struggle to live against the darkness of the unknown. Humans make the best of what they have been given and triumph over shortcomings, shortages, and shortness.

Some forms of Buddhism elaborated the Buddha's teachings into mythopoetic stories that recaptured the security and illusion of earlier religions, but Zen turned away from this tendency and merged instead with the intuitive truth of philosophical Taoism. Zen and haiku sit like two retired ladies on a bus to eternity, each one silently nodding at the other as the many sights pass by. Zen recognizes beauty as more fundamental than emotion, more expansive than any system of thought, more essential than language. We, as writers, have the privilege of taking that fundamental bedrock of beauty and mining it for the ore of words, manufacturing a poem or story like a jade bracelet or a pearl earring. Our creation is not possible without the outside element, the world of existence. We carve it or set it or sometimes just select it, and in so doing bring it to attention, where it glows with the beauty of existence.

Back in the bleachers I put down my book as the game begins again. At the next break I take out my notebook and write:

CHARITY BASKETBALL
EACH TEAM FINDS THE FOUNTAIN
AN AWKWARD HEIGHT

Wright composed his haiku in the late 1950s, right around the same time other popular authors were discovering the form for the first time. Jack Kerouac published his exploration of haiku and Zen in his 1958 autobiographical novel *The Dharma Bums*, which continued the success of *On the Road*, both books sharing many similarities to Basho's travelogues. Wright, Kerouac, and many other new enthusiasts of haiku and Zen recognized the power of this shortest of all forms of poetry to change how the writer saw the world and ultimately how the writer interacted with it. They embraced what they perceived to be the essence of the form—a detached objectivity focused on moment-by-moment existence. Here is one of Kerouac's haiku:

THE PINE WOODS
MOVE
IN THE MIST

This haiku echoes a famous Zen story about two monks watching a flag moving in the wind. One monk said, "The flag is moving." The other said, "The wind is moving." The Sixth Patriarch was passing by, overheard their argument, and said, "Not the wind, not the flag; mind is moving."

In Kerouac's poem we see first the pine woods, then movement, then mist. The simple act of seeing is brought into view. We see "seeing," and further we see our own perception. Then the pines, the mist, the perception, all change. In that realization we briefly glimpse the stillness that is beneath all movement.

From the perspective of our Western literary tradition, muddled as it is with years of higher literary criticism, these erudite and sometimes abstruse meanings are only speculative secondary possibilities. The scholar might remark, "At best, haiku are clever wordplay or romanticized portraits of nature. In these short poems, the arrangement of lines determines the way each image is perceived, and by juxtaposing two incongruous images, they both can be seen in a new way. When a moment is captured by a *haijin* [writer of haiku] it has a photographic quality, but there is no movement of the camera, no rotation to reveal the ugly side; it is an idealized vision glowing with beauty but artificial in its composition and safeguarded by its brevity."

To this cool assessment I answer, "Too true." That is exactly what haiku are, juxtaposed romanticized nature poems. But the form has maintained itself because it has an ancient gyroscope, first set in motion by Basho but spun faithfully down the centuries, that keeps the form fresh, keeps it from devolving into ditties, or from developing into academic exercises. The robust nature of haiku, year after year, survives experimentations such as the introduction of the author into the poem, as Kerouac was wont to do, and the reduction of the form to one or two words, as exemplified by some writers from the late 1990s. What accounts for its sturdy persistence, its time-independent effectiveness? Some styles come and go—even the ancient Japanese form of poetry called *tanka* is seeing a revival these days—but the sublime and mind-expanding haiku is unrivaled the world over as a vehicle for conveying wonder and beauty. The secrets of this form can complement all styles of writing, and hop around any old genre until it reverberates with the same throaty music as these frog-voiced poems.

Japanese Beauty

There are four types of beauty in Japan: *hade, jimi, iki,* and *shibui. Hade* is the beauty of youth, the beauty of singers, actors, and performers. Bright, audacious, covered in bangles, it is the beauty furthest from wabi sabi.

Jimi is the beauty of sober colors, traditional treatments, and correct style. It is long wearing, trustworthy, and clean. It is the beauty of the establishment. It is reliable and pleasant without any aspirations beyond function.

Iki is the stylish sophisticated beauty that jimi is not. *Iki* literally means something that is pure, like a plant essence. It is a processed sort of purity, the purity of refined soap or a well-designed machine. Originally, it was a kind of high-spirited feeling, a manly pride, and a confident spirit. It came to refer to refined manners and appearance. It is the beauty of a clever and witty diplomat, the beauty of modern cities, the beauty produced in assembly lines to exacting standards. It is not usually showy like hade, but instead relies on its quality ingredients and quality control. It doesn't boast, because it is simply the best there is and anyone with any education will recognize it. It is a beauty of engineers and technicians and politicians. Iki men are decisive, assertive, and polished. Iki women are confident, wear their sexuality with pride, but use their sex appeal with careful deliberation. Iki is like "hade grown up" and playing with the big boys. It has a price tag. It is a beauty with a label. Look for it in beauty magazines and chic furniture stores. The movers and shakers in the interior design business would like to make wabi sabi the next iki trend, but it will be a tough job because real wabi sabi is shibui.

Shibui is recognized by its ability to evoke a feeling of tranquility. Shibui is subdued, modest, and humble, yet it has an earthy integrity that calls for a second look. It is the kind of beauty the tea masters sought. The old Japanese character for shibui has a line that signified water and three of the characters that mean "to stop." Shibui blocks water, retains the eye, arrests attention, confronts the palate. Examples of shibui are the bitter taste of powdered green tea, the astringent quality of an unripe persimmon, the rough texture of a weathered barn. It may be fresh from the garden or naturally aged, but it is never overly refined. It can be complicated on the tongue but not complicated in ingredients. It is the most difficult of the beauties to explain and the least talked about because it relies on intuition. You just know it looks right. It is blue jeans and a T-shirt on a clean unadorned body. It is a bed of irises all the same color. It is just the right amount of something, especially if that amount is one authentic original thing. Ralph Waldo Emerson captured the essence of shibui when he said, "We ascribe beauty to that which is simple; which has no superfluous parts; which exactly answers its end; which stands related to all things; which is the mean of many extremes." Decorators with an eye for shibui tend to remove and remove and remove until there are only primary lines and shapes and then an object is chosen to balance the room. That object is valued for its significance as much as for its proportion and color. Something old is better than something new. It evokes longing for balance. Trends, the latest fashion, the popular style, and perfect arrangements have little shibui in them. A shibui room brings out deep conversation; a shibui woman draws out a thoughtful man; a shibui man listens to a thoughtful woman; a shibui child is a rare child indeed. Shibui is marked by three main characteristics: wabi, sabi, and yugen.

Aware, Sabi, and Karumi

In the mid-eighth century, just before the beginning of the Heian period, some 4,500 poems were collected in a book called the *Collection of Myriad Leaves*. This collection is considered by many to be one of the finest collections of poems ever put together. Sam Hamill suggests that the poets represented in the *Collection* of *Myriad Leaves* express the themes and emotional sensibility that are the foundation upon which all subsequent Japanese poetry was built. These poets are admired for their uncluttered, direct, and sometimes wrenching expression of emotion. Here is an example from this time period that represents for me the combination of observation and expression that made these poems powerful:

> In the evening they paddle by the reeds,
> in the morning they dive offshore,
> these wild ducks sleep close by their mates,
> and cross their wings to keep the frost off their tails,
> white as the paper tree, they brush it away.

> As water flows and does not return,
> as wind blows and is not seen,
> so my wife who was of this world died and is gone,
> nothing of her is left.

> I spread the clothes she made for me to wear,
> and lie alone.

In this poem the poet, Tajihi, describes two wild ducks and without mentioning the season or the temperature gives us a clear sense that these two creatures share companionship during the day and warmth on a winter evening. This clear familiar image is followed by abstract images of the flow of water and the blowing of wind. Then we are confronted with the pivotal moment in the poem when we realize that the cool tone of the water and wind are precursors to the poet's own coolness at the loss of his wife. By describing how he spreads out the clothes his wife made for him he echoes the ducks crossing their wings to keep off the frost. This poem is sensitive and tender, expressing clearly the Japanese aesthetic of *aware* (pronounced "ah wah ray"). *Aware* means sensitivity or emotional receptivity and usually has a sorrowful quality.

Basho read and appreciated the poems in this collection and was familiar with the importance of *aware*. After Basho's time a major scholar, Motoori Norinaga (1730–1801), carefully scrutinized the collection and concluded that the quality unifying these poems was a sensitivity to things in nature and the transient beauty of such things. He coined the phrase *mono no aware*, "sensitivity to things," and declared this concept to be absolutely central to the Japanese national character.

Basho had also understood the centrality of *mono no aware* but did not make it the main element of his own poetic style. He chose sabi instead because it had a subtly different tone. Both sabi and *aware* have to do with loneliness and solitude, but while *aware* progresses to sorrow, Basho saw that sabi progresses to acceptance and appreciation. For Basho, sabi had something similar to but not identical with tranquility. This something was a sort of courageous acceptance of life with all its trials and joys. It was a willingness to live with memories and feelings without being driven by them.

He told a student that sabi was the color of a poem and gave an example of an elderly man dressing in his vintage military uniform to visit an old battlefield, or of an aged servant putting on his finest clothes to serve his young master at a banquet. Sabi expresses this pluckiness or unwillingness to give up. It borders on noble but is saved from the pomp of nobility by wabi, which produces a humility about the whole affair. I think this is why Basho used the two terms together. He recognized that the awareness and fortitude that come with maturity can go to a person's head and so insisted on a wabi sensibility. To me this is the strength of wabi sabi.

If you can really let it mold you, or express itself through you, you will produce stories and essays that achieve this quality. Ask yourself, "How do I remain open to the realities of life and death and lead my readers to wabi sabi instead of despair?" For Buddhists, openness to the realities of life, seeing things as they really are, inevitably leads to a realization that the world is full of loss and pain. The Buddha's solution to this problem of pain, the eightfold path, involves the practice of nonattachment. Basho was surely familiar with this path but chose a different one. He chose what he called the "Way of Elegance." This path led him to develop a style called *shofu*, which flowed with *karumi*, or lightness. Here are five poems that Basho wrote that remain open to the reality of life while at the same time lead to sabi and light:

THE MORNING'S SNOW
I CAN CHEW DRIED SALMON
ALONE

SORROW—
BENEATH THE OLD HELMET
A CRICKET CHIRPS

A CURTAIN OF COLD RAIN
OBSCURES MOUNT FUJI—
BEAUTY FILLS WITH QUESTIONS

WITH EACH GUST OF WIND
THE BUTTERFLY PICKS A NEW SPOT
ON THE WILLOW

THIS ROAD:
NO ONE TO GO WITH
AUTUMN DUSK

Karumi was the hallmark of Basho's mature style. I was surprised to find it hidden in Thoreau's advice to himself. As far as I know, Thoreau never read Basho, yet written on the inside cover of one of his journals from 1855 are these notes to himself:

"My faults are:

- Paradoxes,—saying just the opposite,—a style which may be imitated.
- Ingenious.
- Playing with words,—getting the laugh,—not always simple, strong, and broad.
- Using current phrases and maxims, when I should speak for myself.
- Not always earnest.
- 'In short,' 'in fact,' 'alas!' etc.
- Want of conciseness."

It is amazing to find similar counsel from two different men who shared a desire to "get at the marrow" of life and express it in their writing. They both concluded that clever wordplay and impressive language were not what was needed. They sought direct, earnest, genuine expression. Basho added to this the need to not take himself too seriously, to hold the reigns gently, and smile knowingly at what could make him cry. The world needs writers like this.

Poetry in All Kinds of Writing

Basho was a poet. Writing poetry is sometimes described as a process of capturing the essence of a thing, a person, an event, something, anything; securing it down on the page with such brevity that the mind awes, delights in the upwelling of emotions.

Poetry satisfies and sometimes verifies our longings by revealing them, flecks of gold in the prospector's pan. This swishing away of the sand and bark and debris to leave the heavy shiny immutable source of our joy was what Basho loved. The process was satisfying, the way of life pleasurable. Seeing what is, bracing oneself against the onrush of insight, fills a mind with wilderness, unrecognized depth, and the poet is touched by his own role in the magnification of such beauty. To boil down a perception, skim off the foam of superfluous words—that was Basho's ongoing work. Poetry is generally short, or broken into short lines. The poet uses selection and exclusion to focus attention, to juxtapose words and images in uncommon ways and thereby amplify sharp feelings of appreciation or wonder or to trigger thoughtfulness and reflection. These techniques can complement many forms of writing, and will be highlighted in Chapter 8.

Five

Enlightenment:

lose yourself in writing
with a language
older than words

UNDER THE STREET LAMP

EACH SNOWFLAKE

MERGES WITH ITS SHADOW

Writer: "What is the connection between enlightenment and writing?"

Basho: "Art can be a path to enlightenment because it brings your whole attention to what you are doing. When you focus on writing you forget yourself; you lose yourself in the flow of words. This leads to poetry."

Writer: "Is poetry the best kind of writing?"

Basho: "Real poetry is to live a beautiful life. To live poetry is better than to write it."

Writer: "How do we live poetry?"

Basho: "Poetry is the real self. The illusory self is what you think of when you say, 'I am a poet.' It actually has no independent existence; it is as impermanent as everything else. A role model for me in letting go of the illusory self was the priest Saigyo. He was obedient to and at one with nature. He lived his poetry. It is an elegant way; I call it the Way of Elegance."

Writer: "Is the real self the soul?"

Basho: "Everything we do has an influence upon the real self. The real self, the everlasting self, is poetry. You find the real self by living and writing poetry."

Writer: "Is the real self God?"

Basho: "An enlightened person sees a flash of lightning and doesn't think, 'I could have been killed.' An enlightened person sees a flash of lightning and loses herself in it. The beauty fills her with poetry. You can't dwell on your own fate when you are full of poetry."

Enlightenment and Writing

Enlightenment is important to a wabi sabi writer in two ways.

> 1. Writing can trigger enlightenment in the writer. The habit of noticing wabi sabi moments and turning them into poetry is key to this process.

> 2. Your writing can trigger enlightenment in readers. Haiku masters say that linguistic forms can frame images in such a way that a reader will experience an "Aha!" moment.

Writing for Enlightenment

Two terms in Zen describe awakening: *kensho* and *satori*. *Kensho* is glimpsing the illusionary nature of the separate self, a perception that may be lost without continued practice. *Satori* is seeing the nature of all things. Satori is not lost. Basho discovered that the haiku moment could be a form of awakening similar to kensho. It was a shift in perception that might be small and amusing or deep and profound and that, like kensho, might or might not have a transformative effect. In the process of writing we wake up. A writer is receptive. Receptivity is essential to the kind of awakening that Basho discovered.

Basho considered Chuang Tzu to be an important guide in this process of writing poetry. Chuang Tzu, generally considered the second most influential teacher of Taoist philosophy, lived sometime before 250 B.C.E. in a China dominated by the teachings of Confucius and his disciples. Taoism is older than Confucianism, but the usefulness of Confucianism gained popularity quickly and provided a stable foundation for Chinese culture that has lasted to this day. If Confucianism was a scholarly and disciplined approach to ethics and human affairs, Taoism, the philosophy of Chuang Tzu, was an attempt to harmonize individuals with the flow of nature. Basho recognized his own wandering after poetry as part of the Tao. It served no purpose and so was useless, but it increased awareness.

The Useless Tree

Chuang Tzu's logical Confucian friend Hui Tzu said wryly to him, "I have this stinking big tree, the one they call the Tree of Heaven because it usually grows so tall. But this one I have has a trunk so gnarled and bumpy there is no piece from which you could get a straight plank. Even the branches twist so often and at such angles that no tool could make use of any of them. If it were planted by the road with a giant 'Free' sign nailed on it, no carpenter would look twice at it. Your words, Chuang Tzu, are like that tree, big and useless."

Chuang Tzu smiled at his friend and said, "Maybe you've never seen a bobcat or a weasel. Those predators crouch down and hide, watch for something to come along. They leap and race back and forth, this way and that, so focused on their prey that they fall into the fur trader's trap and die hungry. You want to talk big? Consider the yak, big as a storm darkening the sky, yet it doesn't know the first thing about catching prey. Finally, let's look at that big tree that bothers you with its uselessness. Why don't you plant it at a children's camp, or out in the wilderness where the monks are? Then go and wander around it, or lie down under it and fall asleep. Axes will never shorten its life, nothing can ever harm it. Doesn't that useless tree avoid the snares of usefulness?"

Thomas Merton said that Chuang Tzu was speaking to a culture of people who believed in the supremacy of usefulness. Do you find yourself in a similar culture? Are you valued by how much effort you put into your education, job, or moral development, by how much dedication you show to your family and other duties?

Chuang Tzu reminded Hui Tzu of the Tao, suggested a balance that had been known but forgotten. He teased his Confucian friend with a re-examination of what is useful in life. The Confucian way of looking at a tree was to see how many boards could be efficiently cut from it; the Taoist way of looking at the same tree was to see that even in deformity and apparent uselessness there can be value, maybe a higher value. Wabi sabi finds beauty and value in the old, useless, and unnoticed. You can be like Chuang Tzu and tell stories to your readers that help them see the value of things they have not thought to value, see a different perspective on common objects assumed to be worthless, and see the value of overlooked ideas. How did Chuang Tzu discover the value of uselessness? Basho, after years of considering this question, decided that Chuang Tzu simply observed without preconceptions and assumptions, without the established views held by his family, friends, and the wider culture.

Be a Yak

Confucianism teaches that a "superior person" masters four virtues—compassion, duty, love, and wisdom—and obtains this mastery through obedience to the Tao. This system of moral development is a complex structure of duties and rituals that requires a lifelong effort to perfect. Confucius himself did not achieve perfection until he was seventy. In this state of perfect understanding and practice, he "followed the ways of his heart without breaking any rules." Confucianism, however, ran into a problem that is inherent in any system of moral education: People tend to imitate a virtue or a virtuous person rather than embrace the virtue itself. Teachers have a hard time knowing how to help students embrace a virtue without coercion, so more often than not, they resort to coercion. They do this because they know by experience that in many cases students can "fake it till they make it." While this may be true, and while there is a certain pleasure in following a path laid out before you, there is also a tendency for people to fake it till they get good at faking it. Even worse, there is a tendency for people to think that if they are good at faking it, they are good. This is what Chuang Tzu criticized in the Confucians and also, interestingly, what Jesus criticized in the Pharisees. Neither Jesus nor Chuang Tzu was criticizing the virtues of the established schools; they were criticizing the tendency of powerful people within these systems to think they had achieved enlightenment and moral perfection, when in fact all they had achieved was semblance of both.

Chuang Tzu's advice to his friend to visit the useless tree in a useless location and do nothing was a way of saying that in seeking usefulness, he might fall prey to the fur trader's snare and be left naked of skin, stripped of life. That can happen to people who only imitate virtue. The world of winners and losers fosters imitators; it rewards those bobcats and weasels who run and run until they are caught. How much harder it is to be a yak or a twisted tree; to be, as it were, a nonparticipant sitting on the sidelines.

As a wabi sabi writer, you will find you are a yak from time to time, just sitting, just observing. Be a yak or a twisted tree, useless to the eyes of superior people. Uselessness is full of wabi sabi light. It enlightens. It allows questions about what is important. It allows you to consider the values of your culture, allows you to get outside the assumptions and preconceptions about what is important. When you see what is considered useless by a culture, you see the gaps, the imbalances. Write about that; it has been missed or hidden. Embrace uselessness, and it will reward you with longevity of sight.

Peace of Mind

It is morning and I get up before the rest of the family and shower and dress and make my breakfast. I find a favorite audio book and load it in the CD player. Today I have picked *Zen and the Art of Motorcycle Maintenance* for my breakfast accompaniment. The disk starts at a point where the author is discussing "stuckness." Throughout the previous chapters, the author talked about two ways of knowing, the classical, rational way of science and technology, and the romantic, intuitive way of art and storytelling. This morning's disk considers the problem of stuckness, that point at which you run into a problem you can't solve and for which the instruction manual provides no guidance. The author gives the example of damaging the head of a screw that holds a covering plate to a motorcycle engine so that it cannot be removed. Without the ability to undo that screw and take off the plate, the motorcycle cannot be repaired. Then, he talks about stepping back from classical understanding (the technical knowledge about how the machine works) and stepping back from romantic understanding (the appreciation of the beauty and purpose of the machine).

The author, Robert Persig, explains that what is required is unification of these two understandings into something beyond both. To unify these two ways of knowing, a mechanic must have a state of mind in which "quality" guides the work. The state of such a mind, he says, is peaceful. I stop chewing my toast and listen intently. "The way to see what looks good and to understand the reasons it looks good, to be at one with this goodness as the work proceeds, is to cultivate an inner quietness, a peace of mind so that goodness can shine through. I say inner peace of mind. It has no direct relationship to external circumstances, it can occur to a monk in meditation, to a soldier in heavy combat, or to a machinist taking off that last ten-thousandth of an inch. It involves unself-consciousness which produces a complete identification with one's circumstances. And there are levels and levels of this identification, and levels and levels of quietness quite as profound and difficult of attainment as the more familiar levels of activity."

I take a sip of tea and swallow. Suddenly, the image of a furry creature in a boat jumps into my mind. The furry creature is paddling the boat down a river on another planet. Persig continues, saying that solutions to problems that have stranded you are often found while you just look at the motorcycle without speculation or analysis, or by taking time away from the work to do something else. He gives the example of fishing, sitting by a lake or stream waiting for a fish to come along and bite, waiting for a solution to come along and swim up through the crevices of your mind to awareness. The fish I catch this morning keeps saying, "It involves unself-consciousness, which produces a complete identification with one's circumstances." Vincent van Gogh described the experience this way: "I have a terrible lucidity at moments these days when nature is so beautiful, I am not conscious of myself any more, and the picture comes to me as in a dream."

Makoto Ueda, in his biography of Basho, writes, "Basho had come to perceive a mode of life by which to resolve some deep dilemmas and to gain peace of mind. It was based on the idea of sabi, the concept that one attains perfect spiritual serenity by immersing oneself in the egoless, impersonal life of nature." Sabi, the loneliness that allows for appreciation of and communion with nature, is a way of losing the ego, a way of being in the world unself-consciously. How remarkably similar Ueda's description of Basho's gaining peace of mind is to Persig's description of the mechanic's need for peace of mind. Persig says that peace of mind is the primary goal of a mechanic, the prerequisite to any successful repair project. The same can be said of writing. Peace of mind is the state needed to see into the world in a way that uncovers solutions and insights.

How Huan

Peter Kreeft in his book *C. S. Lewis: A Critical Essay* says that the binding thread of all of Lewis's interest is "a love of concrete things both extraordinary and ordinary. The universe is so rich, full, and fascinating to him that he feels no need to retreat into his own subjectivity . . . the key to Lewis's mind is its . . . outer-directedness." The furry animal paddling a boat that jumped into my mind while listening to Persig is a creature from Lewis's imagination, a furry poet named Hyoi. Since childhood, Lewis was fascinated by the idea of talking animals, other creatures who shared our ability to communicate but who were very different from us, who retained their best animal qualities whole and intact. The Narnia books are filled with animals; not, as some have suggested, for their allegorical utility, but primarily for the sheer love of "animalness." Lewis also filled his space trilogy with talking animals that lived on other planets. The ability to talk, Lewis felt, was an ability that gave rise to awareness. He called this linguistically derived awareness *hnau* (pronounced "now.")

In the space trilogy, a philologist on a walking tour is taken to another planet, where he encounters creatures who look like terrestrial animals but who have hnau. Throughout the course of the trilogy, the reader watches another human character twist hnau into something else. This character is eventually referred to as the un-man, a formidable logician who becomes committed to "improving" and "enlightening" the creatures of other worlds so that they may experience the full range of human freedom, the freedom to think independently and construct alternate realities for themselves, to make up stories. This type of freedom requires thinking not just about what is, but about what might be, and realizing that what might be could be better than what is. Once this concept has been accepted by one of the aliens, a beautiful Eve-like creature called Tinidril, the un-man tempts her to follow her newly acquired storytelling ability and imagine a different relationship with her God. The un-man insists that she can only do this if she disobeys an illogical rule set down by her God. The un-man tells Tinidril that in disobedience she will rise above her current state of hnau and obtain a level of awareness she has never had before. He argues that the sheer arbitrariness of the command (not to spend the night on the only fixed land on the planet) is a hint to the Deity's wish that she choose, on her own, to disobey. In so doing, she will become her own individual, in control of her own life; she will decide for herself what is good and right. By doing this she will be able to meet her God in a different, better way. Her independence of volition and thought will allow for a deeper relationship with her God.

This argument has been used to explain the Biblical creation story, suggesting that "the fall" was necessary to ensure self-awareness; that God does not want humans to be unconscious automatons who react on the basis of instinct or fear. By making up our own minds without divine coercion we gain a qualitatively superior experience of life and our Creator. Lewis retells the creation story to highlight this aspect of awakening, and then he suggests an alternative. Will the new Eve choose the level of awareness promised by the un-man and become like us, or will she obey God and retain her "animalness"? In the end, she chooses to obey the rule to stay off the fixed land at night and returns to the floating mats of vegetation that drift around her globe. In so doing, she rises to a new level of hnauness based not on alienation from nature but on a consciously chosen harmony with it.

In this alternative spiritual evolution, we have a beatific image of a hnau-endowed creature who, as Lewis put it, "stepped up where we stepped down." Instead of a fall into individuality,

Tinidril chooses to align herself with a divine purpose that carries her to a state of awareness beyond individuality. Her floating mats of vegetation are a striking image of a floating world (the term used by literati to describe Japan) where a person is carried along by the forces of nature in obvious and tangible ways. The mats remind her that everything changes. Lewis suggests that in this choice to be obedient Tinidril finds a way of living that is more satisfying and natural than what the un-man recommended. She follows the Tao; she aligns herself with its mystery and progresses without effort into her new awareness. Lewis was familiar with Taoism and wrote a book called *The Abolition of Man* in which he argued that moral values exist as part of the Tao.

Tinidril's Approach

A protest that sometimes goes up in response to Lewis and his picture of obedience to the Tao is that there really is value in individuality that seems lost in obedience. Lewis would respond that if individuality is an important quality, it will not be outside the Tao. Individuality is not the problem he is pointing to; it is choosing to do something against the way, against the natural flow of things. The Song philosopher Cheng Hao said, "In quiet contemplation, one finds all things have their own reasons for existence." Roman stoic Epictetus said, "True instruction is this: to learn to wish that each thing should come to pass as it does." This is what Tinidril chose. Thoreau called it "living deliberately," by which he meant going into nature with his eyes and ears open, ready to hear and see the unexpected. Thoreau noted that formal education pales in comparison to what he calls the "discipline of looking always at what is to be seen." He describes sitting in his doorway all morning listening to and watching nature in a kind of reverie. "I did not read books the first summer; I hoed beans. Nay, I often did better than this. There were times when I could not afford to sacrifice the bloom of the present moment to any work, whether of the head or hands. I love a broad margin to my life."

This experience is rare and, as all rare things are, precious. In fully unfolded moments we see what is to be seen. We penetrate past illusion, preconception, expectation, and indoctrination. To look at something as it is, to look at all things as they are, is enlightenment. The Zen Master Dogen said, "Life is nothing more than searching for and acting out the myriad possibilities of meaning with which the self and the world are pregnant." He and his followers believed that everything points toward what needs to be known; the rocks, the trees, the streams, the people, everything pointing the way. To access this knowledge, sit openly in their presence and allow yourself to hear the language beyond words. Follow these sages' advice in your writing and you will record this deeper language.

Roshi John Daido Loori observed that the awakening that occurs in nature takes place through a sort of language he calls "intimate talk." Intimate talk brings the teacher out of the student, rather than bringing a student to a teacher. The teacher is available to everyone and teaches with a language more direct than words. This language is not debate or dialogue, not communication at all really; it is like the sound of a waterfall rolling stones in a deep dark pool; there is a message, but no words. This is the Tao, a stream of language without words that illuminates by being and illuminates all beings. It is what Norman Maclean alludes to in his story *A River Runs Through It* and what Dickens refers to in his book *Dombey and Son* when young Paul says, "I want to know what it says, the sea Floy, what is it that it keeps on saying?" Paul's sister Florence replies that "it is only the sound of the rolling waves." "Yes, but I know that," Paul says. "They are always saying something, always the same thing."

Thomas Merton identified this way of communing with nature and listening to its intimate talk as the central ingredient in a contemplative's life. He wrote, "Life is very simple: We are living in a world that is absolutely transparent to God and God is shining through it all the time. This is not just a fable or a nice story. It is true. If we abandon ourselves to God, and forget ourselves, we see it sometimes, and we see it maybe frequently. God shows everywhere, in everything—in people and in things and in nature and in events." Writing about Chuang Tzu, Merton noted that the Taoist philosopher seeks to abandon the need to win anything or procure anything, not insight, wisdom, or even enlightenment. The desire to win or obtain something is unhelpful because enlightenment is not a thing; it is a realization without form. The desire to win or succeed divides a person's attention, be she an archer or a potter, a tea master or a writer. The writer who flows with the Tao, who observes and transmutes her observations in a way that illuminates others, can amplify the process by following Basho's suggestion to write down the intimate talk. Take Tinidril's approach, stay off the fixed land, return to the moving mats of vegetation, the growing islands of obedience to the Tao. They are where wabi sabi is; they will sustain you.

Attachment

Dr. Gerald Grow in his article "Buddhism—A Brief Introduction for Westerners" summarizes the traditional Buddhist understanding of suffering this way: "Suffering arises because everything changes, everything is impermanent. Everything is in process, all the time. Whenever we hope to find any lasting happiness by means of something that is changing, suffering results." The essential truth of this statement is recognized by anyone who examines the things in life that make them happy. It may be a spouse or partner, a child, an object, or an idea. Having these things brings meaning, security, and fulfillment. If they are taken away, the meaning, security, and fulfillment are lost.

Wabi sabi acknowledges three things: "nothing is perfect, nothing lasts, and nothing is finished." So, at first glance, it seems to celebrate the very thing that causes suffering. Yet, Basho found that wabi sabi led to enlightenment. So what is going on here? Basho himself studied Zen for several years and traveled in disguise as a Zen priest, yet he clearly became attached to people and places, wept openly beside ancient battlegrounds and other sites of romance or valor. He suffered gladly the pains of attachment and sympathy, identified with nature and its pathos. Either he was not very disciplined in his Buddhist practice, or he understood something about attachment and loss that we could do well to learn.

Carol Shields in an interview about her book *Unless* said, "Family is the true subject of the novel. . . . Every novel is about a child finding her way home." Perhaps finding that the journey *is* home? Many novels are about dysfunctional homes in which healthy attachment is missing, but somewhat fewer explore healthy family relationships in which attachment functions well. Shields said that she deliberately intended to portray a happily married couple in *Unless,* and she succeeded without being smarmy. She did this by presenting characters in relationships of attachment, showing that one family member's suffering affects everyone else.

In *Unless,* the character Reta Winters tells her story of loss. She is attached to her oldest daughter, Norah, who has mysteriously left college and boyfriend to sit on a street corner with a sign around her neck that reads, "goodness." Reta and her family and friends speculate about the cause of Norah's withdrawal from society, and Reta remembers a pivotal conversation she had with her daughter the day before Norah abandoned life for her silent sitting amidst the traffic of the city. Norah said that she loved the world more than she could any one person; that literature, travel, language, every little footpath in India and movement of the tides drew her interest.

Norah's desperation in the face of the bigness of the universe, her longing to draw it all into her awareness, her desire to stretch herself wide enough to take it all in, is a desire for attachment. After Norah's descent into empty sitting, Reta says, "She is too busy with her project of self-extinction." The self can sometimes do that, fizzle like a candle guttering in the storm of existence. Norah's sudden break from her longing for the whole world, to her silent and cold resignation from it all, seems tragic, and we search for some other way for Norah, and for ourselves, to deal with the existential crisis of human finiteness. Through the course of the novel, we see Norah's family try to connect to her, to bring her back from her remote hermitage of the mind.

Dr. Lynken Ghose in his article "A Study in Buddhist Psychology: Is Buddhism Truly Pro-Detachment and Anti-Attachment?" explores the popular interpretation of Buddhist teachings about attachment and detachment and suggests that it may fall short of a full understanding of the original texts. He calls for a re-examination of the idea of removing all attachments in order to attain enlightenment. Ghose points out that attachment and detachment are themselves concepts that we are tempted to cling to. Attachment and detachment are dualities that frame human suffering. Children and adults alike need healthy attachment in order to grow into healthy individuals, but overattachment to any individual, object, or idea leads to problems.

John Bowlby and the attachment theorists that followed him conducted experiments that revealed that secure attachments in early childhood allow for confident exploration later in life.

Uncertainty and insecurity regarding a child's primary caregiver, on the other hand, can lead to maladaptive behaviors. One of these maladaptive behaviors is emotional detachment. Detachment in this sense is a kind of a coping technique a person uses to deal with pain and fear. Even someone who has been well attached to her family for years can experience a trauma that disconnects her. This is what happens to Norah. To avoid the pain of a traumatic experience, an experience her family doesn't learn about until much later, she detaches from everyone and everything she knows. Through the efforts of her loving family, she finally wakes and attaches once again to the people she loves.

Writing to Trigger Enlightenment

When I was thirteen I watched an animated TV version of C. S. Lewis's *The Lion, the Witch, and the Wardrobe*. My mother noticed my interest and mentioned that we had the whole Narnia book series. I proceeded to read one each night for a week. When I finished them I went on to Lewis's space trilogy, discovered Tolkien, and read on through several genres and several thousand authors. *The Lion, the Witch, and the Wardrobe* was the beginning of my reading life, and some of those early stories are still with me, still working their way through my subconscious, informing me at odd times about the world and my place in it. I experienced "flow reading" for the first time with that book, a type of reading in which I entered a state of flow and became so immersed in the story that I forget about time and my surroundings; forgot, in fact, about myself. The Harry Potter series had the same effect on my children. These trigger books fire people like a bullet into a completely different world of imagination and ideas from which they return as a space traveler returns to earth. They have enjoyed their journey away but find the earth more precious than they had ever known before.

Colin Brown, one of my writing professors, used to say that people read to learn something new, even and perhaps especially when they read fiction. Newness is what they are after, he said, and writers should look for newness everywhere, even in themselves. Thirty-three people responded to a recent survey I conducted online, and the top three reasons given for reading books were:

1. To lose yourself in a story

2. To see things from a different perspective

3. To gain insight

Stories like *Unless* model enlightenment in their characters and provide examples of how we who are writers can give our readers this gift.

six

Motivation:
imitate a yak and share
something wild

WAITING TO TURN

A THISTLE SEED

MOVES WITH THE TRAFFIC

Writer: "Basho, did you ever have a hard time finding the motivation to write?"

Basho: "There was a time when I struggled with motivation. I thought I had discovered in poetry a way to move from sabi to enlightenment. Sabi was the key; it contained an acceptance of things as they are. In the middle of my life I hit a rough patch that challenged this. Perhaps I was overly attached to poetry, believing it could do more than it can. But when I sat with hardship as a gift, the poetry came through. I found that I could be attached to what I loved and still hold it with an open hand, always ready to let it go. This is the only way I found to stay connected with people and places and not get trapped by my own desire to hold on to them. Travel taught me that there is always a new person to meet, a new sight to see, new inspiration at the next bend in the road. There is no need to hang on to beauty and goodness; there will be more to come. Writing gives you a chance to make impressions of what you love and share them. I could give up everything except that, except the sharing. That is what motivated me."

Six Traits

There was a wabi sabi man who struggled to express what he loved and who chronicled his struggles for his brother in a series of letters that allow us to see into his inner world. His name was Vincent van Gogh. This artist was rejected and ignored during his lifetime but he kept painting through isolation, poverty, and illness. Van Gogh exhibited six traits in his life that are worth considering:

1. Perseverance. His art was unique and original but no one recognized it at the time. Nevertheless, he developed his own style through years of effort.

2. Wabi sabi. It is difficult to find one of his paintings that does not convey wabi sabi beauty. He understood the beauty of the ordinary, the hidden value of the every-day. He uncovered both its loneliness and the way it binds people to a place. He chose wabi sabi models for his art, simple farmers and miners authentically portrayed in their natural settings.

3. Simplicity. He lived simply and worked diligently to capture what he saw, forgoing a prosperous life for his art.

4. Expressiveness. He not only painted but he also wrote what he thought and felt about his work. He highlighted his writing with sketches and delighted in sharing beauty.

5. Independence. He lived his convictions in poverty, unappreciated and unrecognized, because he knew what he was trying to achieve. Like everyone else, he worried about his physical needs and wished he were in a better position financially, but his convictions and his strong sense of the value of his own perceptions allowed him to enter into the painting process with abandon.

6. Courage. He faced with resolution the exclusion he experienced from painterly society. He invited painters to visit him, sent correspondences to those he respected, and sought help for his illness, all while producing painting after painting.

Van Gogh lived a heroic life, and his story inspires me to continue writing when the rewards seem far away.

Perseverance

Van Gogh sold one painting in his lifetime, *The Red Vineyard*. One hundred years after his death, a portrait he painted of his doctor, *Portrait of Dr. Gachet*, sold in auction at Christie's for $82.5 million, the highest price ever paid for a painting at that time. Later that year, his pen-and-ink rendering *Garden with Flowers* sold in a Christie's auction for $8.6 million, the highest price ever paid for a drawing. What does this tell us about his art? It tells us that something about his work was significant enough to draw the attention of art collectors. It also reveals something about the fickle nature of the wealthy people who pay these prices for art.

Van Gogh's paintings are often purchased now for some rather un–wabi sabi reasons. They are good investments. They are prized objects displayed by collectors to impress friends, just like the expensive tea utensils that were used for the same purpose before the development of wabi tea. Owning one of Van Gogh's paintings allows a collector to share in the limelight of the artist. For some collectors, the paintings are valued for a more noble reason, because they represent something about the human journey; they mark a change in the way we see things. If a collector purchases a Van Gogh because he or she sees how unique it is, sees a bit of what Vincent himself saw and tried to share with the rest of us, then perhaps the pomp and ceremony surrounding the purchase of these canvases is tolerable. It is tragic that Van Gogh never received the encouragement he deserved or the financial compensation his work warranted, but it is inspiring that he continued to paint in spite of his tragic circumstances.

In the letters to his brother, Vincent's keenest and sometimes only supporter, we find a deep well of encouragement. Van Gogh's earnestness, genuine compassion, and pure intentions filled his life with shades of childhood. And these qualities tumble out of his letters with the thump and soil of freshly dug potatoes. We learn that Vincent experienced both times of blockage and times when his art flowed almost effortlessly. In the year before his death, during his most productive and inspired period, we find this remarkable sentence in a letter to his brother: "I wish you could spend some time here, you would feel it after a while, one's sight changes: you see things with an eye more Japanese, you feel colour differently. The Japanese draw quickly, very quickly, like a lightning flash, because their nerves are finely tuned, their feeling uncluttered. I am convinced that I shall set my individuality free simply by staying on here."

Practice

What Vincent van Gogh experienced at that time in his life was a combination of love for the place (Arles) and the maturation of his talent through years of practice. The techniques and forms of his art had become like reflexes responding directly to the landscape. He talked of "letting my brush go . . . ," allowing all he had learned and practiced to guide his creative response in an unhindered flow of expression directly onto the canvas. He no longer needed to concentrate on technique or form and so was able to produce some of his greatest canvases. This process of transmuting a place, an image, a person, or a subject through an artistically honed mind and body onto the canvas or page allows the perspective of the artist to burn brightly. In a letter a few days later Vincent wrote, "Is it not emotion, the sincerity of one's feeling for nature, which draws us, and if the emotions are sometimes so strong that one works without knowing one works, when the strokes come with a continuity and a coherence like words in a speech or a letter, then one must remember that it has not always been so, and that in a time to come there will again be hard days, empty of inspiration."

While this quote may hint at Vincent's mental illness (bipolar disorder seems to be the current diagnosis), the experience is recognized to varying degrees by most writers and artists. There are times when we are inspired and times when we are not. What is important to learn from Van Gogh is that when he faced a lack of inspiration he went out in search of it, and would tramp around the countryside with his easel and paints until something caught his eye. I discussed such tramping after beauty in Chapter 2, and it is a technique that *haijin* have known for generations. They call it a *ginko*, or a walk for inspiration.

The most debilitating aspects of Van Gogh's mental illness occurred toward the end of his life. Part of the tragedy was that the mastery he achieved through the internalization of technique and perspective was most developed at the same time his mental illness became incapacitating. Rather than seeing his mental illness as either a cause of or a contributing factor to his art, I think it should be seen as a complicating factor that shortened his life and caused him suffering. When I read his letters from that period of his life, I see a man battling gallantly to maintain his identity and humanity, using his art to focus and stabilize his mind. He knew he was ill, knew that he needed help, and he knew that his art helped him stay sane. The fact that this courageous battle with his mental illness did not rob him of his talent showed the depth of his commitment to his art. Whatever it is in life that challenges you, be it an illness like Vincent's, or a wayward child, a broken relationship, a disability, a hurtful relative, or an oppressive employer, it can be part of your art and the artful life you form in response to it.

Three Activities

Basho developed his style in response to his journey through loss and loneliness. Like Van Gogh, he felt his emotions deeply and allowed them to inform his poetic vision. Instead of detaching from the things that caused him sorrow and loneliness, instead of developing an indifferent attitude as his Buddhist teachers recommended, he fostered a deep sensitivity both to the things he feared losing or had lost, and to the beauty that redeemed those things from their impermanence. He found he could not stop writing, could not stop appreciating the moments that moved him. This love for the fleeting and ephemeral inspired several of his disciples to follow his example.

There are three activities that renewed Basho's passion for writing: wandering, noticing, and sharing. As you develop your own vision and style, try these practices and see if they help sustain you when you lack motivation.

Wander

I have already talked about wandering, but now I would like to take the wandering in a different direction. When his brother was expecting a child Van Gogh wrote, "Ah, now certainly you are yourself deep in nature, since you say that Jo already feels her child move. It is much more interesting even than landscapes, and

I am very glad that things should have changed so for you." Events like childbirth, coming of age, and death can be inspirational, but sometimes we forget how remarkable these events can be.

John Tallmadge, a man who has taught on the subject of literature and wilderness for years, once took a job in Cincinnati. In his early teaching career he believed "the experience of great literature and the experience of great places (are) all of a piece." But Cincinnati was not known for either its great wilderness or its great literature. How was he going to maintain his motivation to write in a place that was, as he described it, "deep in the Rust Belt"? He likened his move there to a "move into exile" and wondered how he could follow his passion for wilderness and literature while stuck in such an uninspiring place. He had a crisis of motivation and needed to be reminded of Basho's advice to "seek what the great writers sought, rather than following in their footsteps." Contrary to Basho's teaching, Tallmadge had taught his students to read the great nature writers and then seek out the places that had inspired them. Like Basho, he visited the sites of great literary inspiration, but unlike Basho, he believed this to be an essential part of a writer's education. He and his students followed Thoreau to the summit of Mount Katahdin, and they followed Edward Abbey into the maze of the Canyonlands. This formula for inspiration was tried, tested, and true, and yet here he was facing the home of the fictional WKRP radio and the Flying Pig Marathon. In the face of this dismal forecast a baby was born, and she changed John's view of wilderness.

In his book *The Cincinnati Arch: Learning from Nature in the City,* Tallmadge recounts his change of perspective as he learns to see the wilderness first in the birth of, and later through the eyes of, his daughter. In the stunned moments after his daughter's birth Tallmadge writes, "The nurse asked me to step aside so that she could take the basin. 'This must all be routine for you,' I said sheepishly. She looked me in the eye. 'Never,' she said."

If you are going through a pregnancy, or if your spouse or partner is, let it inspire you to write; you may birth two creations at the same time. If your children are grown up and expecting their first babies, let that inspire you. A grandparent's view of the event is as valuable as a parent's, as valuable as a sibling's, friend's, neighbor's. If it is meaningful to you, write about it. You may think that everything that could be written about giving birth has already been written. But as with an empty square that Van Gogh drew, and which I will tell you about in a few pages, context changes things. Your context is completely your own, your way of seeing the world unique. By sharing it with me, by capturing the details that matter to you, by describing the events as you experience them and attaching your own reactions, the events will come alive for me and give me your perspective. The more we share in this way the more we become like that nurse, experiencing the wonder and mystery of each new birth.

Tallmadge realized that his encounter with the wilderness of his own reproduction was as significant as any he had experienced in nature. "I was adrift in time, living totally in the present with all my senses focused and engaged," Tallmadge wrote concerning the days immediately following the birth. "Only in moments of I-Thou encounters in the wilderness, when weeks of hiking had scraped my mind to a poised alertness and some animal or tree had stood forth in radiant personhood, had I ever felt the present as something so solid, so real." This experience of finding awakening without remote locations showed Tallmadge that what he valued, what Basho called wabi sabi, was bigger and more available than he had thought.

Basho experienced a similar crisis of motivation in his own life. The trip he took that would eventually be seen as the climax of his career was followed by some short walks with old friends and disciples in Ueno, Kyoto, and towns on the southern coast of Lake Biwa. He stayed at one friend's house after another and enjoyed a form of seclusion that allowed him to choose his interactions with people. He wrote of this time, "In the daytime an old watchman from the local shrine or some villager from the foot of the hill comes along and chats with me about things I rarely hear of, such as a wild boar's looting the rice paddies or a hare's haunting the bean farms. When the sun sets under the edge of the hill and night falls, I quietly sit and wait for the moon. With the moonrise I begin roaming about, casting my shadow on the ground. When the night deepens, I return to the hut and meditate on right and wrong, gazing at the dim margin of a shadow in the lamplight."

During this period, he worked with two of his favorite pupils on an anthology called *The Monkey's Raincoat*, which contained poems that expressed the aesthetic principles Basho had developed during his northern journey. It was the peak of his career,

and when he returned to Edo in the winter of 1691 he was surrounded by friends and admirers. They built a new hut for him, and
kept him busy with invitations to visit and talk. At the same time,
he opened his hut to people in need, an invalid nephew and an ill
woman named Jutei who Basho had known from his childhood.
Jutei had several young children. Basho was used to the poet's life
of wandering at will across the land socializing with educated and
interesting people; domestic life and the tedium of polite social
engagements sapped his creative drive and cluttered his vision.
He fell into depression and at one point vowed to become a recluse.
He wrote to a friend, "Disturbed by others, Have no peace of
mind." He thought poetry was a way to transcend the cares of the
world, but now domesticity and his own fame brought more cares
than he could surmount by poetry alone. "I tried to give up poetry
and remain silent," he wrote, "but every time I did so a poetic feeling would tug at my heart and a flame would flicker to life in my
mind. Such is the allure of poetry." He could not stop doing what
he had fashioned his whole life around, so he decided to simply shut
his door and lock the world out. "Whenever people come, there is
useless talk. Whenever I go and visit, I have the unpleasant feeling
of interfering with other men's business. Now I can do nothing
better than follow the examples of Sun Ching and Tu Wu-lang,
who confined themselves within locked doors. Friendlessness will
become my friend, and wabi will be my wealth."

His time of seclusion lasted only about a month, but it was
enough for him to meditate and find a solution to his dilemma.
That solution was the principle I discussed in Chapter 4 and

alluded to earlier. *Karumi*, which literally meant a "light beauty with subtlety," was something Basho saw as a higher level of sabi. With karumi, the loneliness of sabi opens into acceptance. This new understanding of sabi allowed him to live in the world without being overwhelmed by its sorrow. I think of Basho there with the rambunctious children, the challenges of dealing with disabilities and illness, and I see a soft smile spread across his features. There was a great unexplored wilderness right in his very home, and a means at hand for exploring it and transmuting it into poetry. By drawing poetry from his busy life, he was able to maintain perspective, able to stand apart from himself and see the humor and the pathos in his own life. With this remarkable new principle, he was able to start writing again. When he shared this insight with his students, they immediately began to emulate him. Not long after, several anthologies, *A Sack of Charcoal*, *The Detached Room*, and *The Monkey's Raincoat, Continued* were published. They all contained poems touched by the light of karumi. These poems are not sentimental "feel good" verse, but clear snapshots of daily life conveyed with a calm, amused acceptance. Karumi arises from sabi when we notice and accept what is.

Notice

Mothers and fathers kneel at the feet of their children, pulling long laces tight, cinching leather around small feet. There is the smell of children, ice, and vending-machine coffee. Escorting my son to the edge of the rink, I watch him skate away, wobbling less today than last time, making his way over the artificial sheet of ice to play a game of hockey at the far end of the rink with friends. There are other skaters here; this is not a hockey-only group. This is a home-schooling activity. My older son, already on the ice, carries on an animated conversation with another boy. My son's long hair covers his face until he flicks his head. Then I see his storytelling smile. He is wrapped in narrative on the slippery surface. His smile makes me smile. In front of me two small girls go by holding hands and I catch the phrase, "That's exactly what she said . . ." I start to turn to make my way into the bleachers to watch the whole scene but am stopped by an energetic grandfather who says loudly, "Where are your skates?" His eyes twinkle.

"I prefer to watch," I say.

"You're missing out on the fun," he counters. I think of Chuang Tzu.

"I haven't skated for a long time," I confess, a useless tree.

"No one will laugh," he says, weaseling me.

"Thanks," I say, "maybe sometime I will." I nod like a yak.

He skates away, shaking his head. I find my favorite seat, alone, away from the crowd, and watch my sons skate, watch moms talk and nod, watch a talented man coach some boys on their skating technique. I take out my notebook and start to write. In a few minutes I am lost in the flow, images from memory crashing into images on the ice. I write a haiku, I write about what I think the woman skating with her daughter is feeling, I write several pages of dialogue for a short story. From time to time, I look up and watch. My life as a watcher is rich; I see things others miss, appreciate relationships from my vantage point in the bleachers.

James Dobson tells a story from childhood about his father. His father would wake James early, before the sun was up, bundle him in layers of warm clothes, carry him into the snowy winter dawn, and tuck him into a quiet pocket of snow beside a frozen creek to watch the morning come to life with winter birds and animals. His father would walk a little farther down the streambed and tuck himself into the whiteness. Dobson remembers those times of shared watching with great fondness. Though no words were exchanged, the message his father was telling him came through loud and clear: This is worth seeing; it is worth being here for this. When I heard this story for the first time, I was deeply impressed and reminded of the gift fathers give when they share what they love with their children. Little James learned an important lesson during those cold mornings, and the only teaching that his father did was to carry him there.

As a writer you have the same privilege that James's father had, of carrying a reader to a special place of beauty. So much of the writing that is held up to be great literature is filled with angst, pain, conflict, and grief. The abiding popularity of the *Titanic* story is one that puzzles me. The last time I checked, the movie based on that historic event is still the largest box-office moneymaker in history. Why is the story of an inadequately designed luxury liner that runs into trouble and sinks, killing hundreds of people in the icy waters of the north Atlantic, so interesting to people? The movie is, of course, well written, well acted, and well produced. It is, according to masses of people who love the movie, compelling.

How do I write about those skating moms in a way that rivals the *Titanic*? For me, the skating moms with their children of all ages, discussing home schooling, raising a family, making ends meet, and getting along with their husbands and parents, are as interesting as the heroic deaths of passengers aboard a historic ship. But I recognize that not everyone finds this to be the case. What makes it interesting for me is the perspective I choose to look at it from. This is the key. This is why wabi sabi is so valuable. By becoming wabi sabi, I forgo the pressures to be "on the ice," forgo the need to do anything but notice and record. By giving up action in favor of noticing I gather the words that precipitate out of noticing, write them with appreciation, fold them into the envelope of shared moments, and stamp it with abandon.

Share

When Van Gogh was still a young man living in England and teaching at a boys' school, he spent his spare time visiting art galleries and museums and reading Charles Dickens and George Eliot. He walked in the streets and sketched the boats along the pier. One time, he sent his brother a small sketch of a city square and a lamppost. It wasn't until I read the description in his accompanying letter that I grasped why this scene was so important to him. It was the view through the window of the school where he taught. It was the view his students saw each morning as they gazed after their departing parents. It was also the view these same boys gazed upon when they were denied supper for misbehaving. The children separated from their parents or going without their dinner touched Vincent's sensitive heart and colored the view with sabi. On rainy days the minister in charge of the school was often in a bad mood, but when Vincent looked out on the rainy street with the lamplight shining off the wet paving stones, he was struck by its beauty, and this, in some way, compensated for the dark temper of the minister and the sadness of the boys. Vincent saw all these events connected to each other and wished to convey this view to his brother. The beauty of the square with the lamppost would not be immediately apparent to a passerby, but in the context of the school the square became beautiful. Vincent couldn't resist sharing it.

If you feel this way about something, no matter how ordinary or mundane, write about it. Try to capture the image and the context that gives the image meaning. If you can present the image and the context for your reader, she will feel the same poignancy. As Vincent developed as an artist, he did things in his paintings to communicate the context, so that, for instance, in *The Potato Eaters* we see a group of peasants in such detail and in such subdued light that we feel the weariness of the old woman; the glimmer of hope, or maybe courage, in the younger woman; the direct, uncomplicated character of the man. The dwelling is dark and close, but each face shines brightly. As your skill with wabi sabi develops, you will paint similar pictures with words.

One time while washing dishes at the kitchen sink in the first cottage we lived in, my wife looked out the window and saw a flock of cedar waxwings. "Richard, look," she called, drying her hands on a towel. There in the mountain ash tree just outside the window was a flock of glossy birds, moving from branch to branch, reaching their bills out to grasp the pulpy red berries. These birds, seen through the old wavy single-paned glass, were beautiful, and she wanted me to see. And I saw, and together we stood and watched them, until suddenly they exploded into flight, all at the same time, away through birch trees toward the lake.

Why do we crave companionship while attending a sunset? What is it that joins hand to hand as an elderly couple walk a woodland trail? Beauty brings us together. Sharing a glimpse of something fine, a taste of something rare, a stream of ephemeral music, binds us into the beauty, improves us with its presence. Someone might choose to paint a picture of those waxwings, another composes a song, still another fashions a ceramic like-ness; it doesn't matter. Even if all we do is call, "Come, look!" or "You have to hear this," or "Take a deep whiff of that!" or maybe just "Taste!" the desire is the same, to share the experi-ence with someone else. This tendency we humans have to want to share a moment of beauty, to want company in our wonder, is the same as the motivation to write.

When the wine lover enthusiastically ritualizes the opening of his latest purchase, pours the aged liquid into a glass, watches me sniff it, waits for me to taste it, waits for me to look up in astonish-ment, he is sharing, and that is his reward. That is my gift to him. He has given me a drink of wine; I have given him satisfaction by being pleased. I validate the time he spent reading, browsing, select-ing. I authorize his effort. I sanction his passion. The woman at the movie store asks me if I liked her last recommendation. "Oh yes,"

I say, "deliciously Victorian." And she knows that her job is more than a paycheck, her life more than putting in time.

As a writer, you can experience this power of sharing in a way that will make your writing of interest to others and keep you going when motivation seems to leave you. The secret is in understanding that the waxwings were the magnet that captured Marilyn's attention and when she showed them to me, I too was drawn to them. Philip Roth said that these magnets keep us writing and that if we are able to transmit the magnet through our writing, it will keep the reader reading.

In a work of fiction, the magnet might be an interesting character or compelling story line. In a work of nonfiction, it might be the key concept or insight. Whatever it is, the writer must attach to it, must stay in touch with its vital power. This is a subtle but essential motivator. The magnet is the source of flow. If a writer experiences flow while writing a piece, chances are the reader will too. Mihaly Csikszentmihalyi, in his book *Good Business*, writes, "The most widely reported flow activity the world over is reading a good book, during which one becomes immersed in the characters and their vicissitudes to the point of forgetting oneself." When a writer has written in a state of flow, followed the magnet throughout, she will produce a work that will flow in her reader. This is the strongest motivation I know.

Seven

Community:

in a group of friends you can write from the heart

LONG AFTER CLASS

WE TALK ABOUT BASHO

HIS CAR THE SAME MAKE AS MINE

Writer: "Basho, how important was community to you?"

Basho: "Throughout my life, I tried to balance solitude and companionship. Solitude taught me to listen, friends taught me to write."

Writer: "Are you referring to the Renga groups?"

Basho: "That was the interest that brought us together, but I am talking about traveling with companions up and down mountains, in and out of temples and guest houses. My friends and students and teachers, all had writing on the mind, we talked and talked and wrote and wrote. There is nothing better."

Writer: "What did you talk about?"

Basho: "All sorts of things, but mostly furyu and how to develop it in our lives. I sought out the 'people of furyu,' journeyed over the land month after month hoping to meet these connoisseurs of poetry."

Writer: "What effect does furyu have on a writer?"

Basho: "The type of navigation a writer develops when she makes her home in the stream is different from that of a writer who makes her home on fixed land. The stream-dweller develops an intuition for avoiding boulders and so has time to admire the landscape. It makes her eccentric."

Writer: "Eccentric?"

Basho: "It takes a long time to develop furyu; it takes trial and error. You try things and see what they do to you, develop your taste, open yourself to the unusual, the different, and the beauty that others miss or overlook. When you travel in the stream you see, taste, feel, experience more, and amass a body of firsthand sensations. Children seldom take immediately to eating mushrooms or certain strong-smelling fish. The texture puts them off or their taste buds are just too young. As a child grows older, she recoils less from unusual experiences and retreats less often to the familiar. By adulthood, if she has been introduced to furyu, she learns to enjoy unusual foods, strange textures, creative combinations; she becomes a little odd—more so if her taste in beauty leans toward wabi sabi. Wabi sabi is the pungent mushrooms and stinky fish of the literary world. Not everyone will embrace it right away. And not everyone will be comfortable with you if you do."

Writer: "So a community of like-minded writers will support you in this pursuit?"

Basho: "Finding fellow writers with your taste or style will take time. When a person has followed the Way of Elegance for a while, she reaches a state where all she wants is to attend to quality moments with focused acceptance. Such a stance is hard to maintain; her family and friends will push her to distraction, pressure her to be normal. If you see her in this situation, enter her sabi, share her wabi. Encourage her to follow furyu with you."

Writer: "And that will be the beginning of community?"

Basho: "If you develop a group around furyu, something important happens. You make real the true self."

Writer: "What is the true self?"

Basho: "The true self is the self beyond your individual ability. It is revealed in community. If the group is in touch with furyu, one person's verse will inspire another to produce a poem with similar beauty. It is a kind of magnification of beauty, one beautiful verse inspiring another, and so on. This experience is hard to duplicate in any other way."

Haijin

Marilyn and I are on the ferry heading to Gabriola Island for a meeting of the western branch of Haiku Canada. It is our first meeting. We are nervous. She is nervous because she is not sure she will have enough in common with writers dedicated to such a specific form of poetry. I am nervous because I have been communicating via e-mail with two of these poets, and they have encouraged me, helped me push deeper into the form. What if their e-mail personas are different from their real selves? We had admired their poems in various journals and haiku publications. We worry that our own writing or knowledge of haiku will be lacking or inferior.

On the ferry, we read some favorite haiku and a brochure about Gabriola Island the woman at the ferry ticket office gave us. She said, "Pictures on the front, details inside, just like

Playboy," and motioned us into lane nine. I muse as I park that writing also exposes us to public scrutiny. Haiku collections are intimate glimpses into people's minds.

The ferry's engine changes pitch, and we look up to see the terminal ahead. My heart skips a beat. The docking of this ferry means there is no turning back. I have been committed to making contact with this group, but the clang of the loading plank on the steel deck says, "There is no way now but forward."

On the island, we progress along a winding road deep into the interior. We seem to relax a bit as the dry fields and ramshackle fences go by. Then from a gravel side road, a small feathered body appears pounding along on its webbed feet—a duck at full tilt. She turns into the road and heads toward us in the other lane. Her wings are held out for balance, her beak is thrust out, and her head pumps forward and backward as she runs. I am afraid she will swerve in front of the car and I put my foot on the brake, but she passes us fast on the left and I hear the slap, slap, slap of her fleshy soles on the asphalt.

"There is a haiku in that," I say and Marilyn smiles. I realize we are acting just like this duck, worked into a flap. We relax a little more and study the map for the final few turns and then we see the house, with lots of cars parked along the road edge.

"I didn't think there would be this many people," Marilyn says.

"Well," I say, trying to stay positive, "maybe we will blend into the crowd more easily this way."

We go inside, faces smiling, hands extended, hugs, our hostess makes us welcome, expertly moves us from one room to the next, introduces us around. I see other nervous smiles. We are not the only newcomers.

After getting to know everyone a bit, we are invited on a *ginko*, a walk for inspiration, and we head from the house to Drumbeg Park, an oceanside provincial park that is also the name of one of the books of *haibun* our hostess has written. We talk about the national haiku society and its plans to produce a yearly journal, something professional and glossy and nice to hold. I like beautiful collections of poetry, especially if one of my poems is included, and I daydream momentarily about what the journal would look like. I am warming up to the idea. The senior poet in our group is casual about the idea, almost dismissive. The subject of money comes up. There are questions about grants, increases of membership fees. The way she talks and walks is comfortable, at ease, confident. With her sensible words, she reminds me of my own values, reminds me that the desire for *iki* can mean the loss of *shabui*. We continue on to the park, talk about favorite ways to use punctuation and about how haiku has changed our lives, has helped us see life more clearly. We talk about Basho and haibun and the possibility of introducing fiction into haiku. I am impressed by these knowledgeable, genuine people who have made poetry important in their lives.

We reach the beach and disperse for some private observation. A family is having a picnic, dogs on leashes lunge at each other, kids call threats to the incoming tide, an old man in a hat like mine points across the bay, at me. I photograph the shadow of a dead branch bending across the sandstone and write a haiku about it. I write a haiku about the man in the hat and the running duck.

On the way back from our ginko we meet up again, and Marilyn talks to a woman who is a copyeditor. I hear their voices relax into familiarity, the binding thread of common experience. They talk about the process and importance of editing, and I listen in. I want my words to be laid out on the page in such a way that a reader will skip along from one to the next without a thought for the words themselves. If a reader stumbles over a word, I want it to be because I intend her to stumble, not because my sentences are awkward. A good editor corrects such mistakes, provides honest feedback, and improves the project with her intuitive sense of what works and what doesn't. A person with natural editing abilities senses a writer's style and suggests changes that improve the work in a way the author would do if she had seen it herself. An editor's work, if it is successful, can go unnoticed. The humility required to make someone else look good is deeply wabi sabi.

Back at the house, we each write our haiku anonymously on large sheets of paper and gather to read and critique them. One poem causes a friendly split in the group over the question of using the word "beloved" in a haiku about a damaged petunia. One haijin suggests dropping the word "beloved" and using a simpler, "my petunia" instead. Others point out that "beloved" heightens the pathos of the poem by raising the significance of the plant from something that is simply beautiful to something invested with emotional attachment. Another haijin points out that the pronoun "her" would change the feel of the poem again.

We are all a little impressed at how these small word changes affect the poem. It frames the poetic process in a different light. I feel how significant poetry is, how important it is to share it, and what a privilege it is to receive these word clusters within a group of people who appreciate them. I think about how nice it would be to bring more people into this circle. Someone talks about inspiration, another about being bitten by the haiku bug, another about writer's block and the value of free writing.

After a casual discussion over dinner we gather again, and one of the leaders of the group reads tanka from a new anthology. There are sighs and expressions of satisfaction around the room. It reminds me of a prayer group. Soon others bring out *haiga* (combinations of visual art and haiku) to share, and too soon it is time to go home.

Traveling in the car back to the ferry, Marilyn and I share our thoughts of the day, and on the ferry we read from some new haiku collections we bought at the meeting. I have a headache and am tired, but feel a light elation. There will be more meetings and more insights. I think about a ninety-three-year-old man who was one of the newcomers at the meeting. One of his poems was truly beautiful. He arrived humble and willing to learn. "Same age as my grandfather," Marilyn remarks. I know he will write some very good poems and I look forward to reading them.

An Immense Solitude

In his book *The Four Loves*, C. S. Lewis notes that when two people discover they read the same books, admire the same artists, or enjoy the same music, it is like finding a long-lost twin. There is an initial burst of joy and then a strong desire to find out if the other person's interest, appreciation, or taste is genuine, or if that person is just faking it. Lewis speculates that early in the human journey an individual might have noticed something others did not, that a deer was beautiful as well as edible, that he liked the hunting as well as the eating. Perhaps he wondered about the stories of gods and hoped that they were holy as well as powerful. Unless such an individual found another with the same questions or insights, nothing would happen. Lewis wrote, "As long as each of these percipient persons dies without finding a kindred soul, nothing (I suspect) will come of it; art or sport or spiritual religion will not be born. It is when two such persons discover one another, when, whether with immense difficulties and semi-articulate fumblings or with what would seem to us amazing and elliptical speed, they share their vision—it is then that friendship is born. And instantly they stand together in an immense solitude."

Why an immense solitude? Because an interest separates the interested from the disinterested. An insight removes the enlightened from the unenlightened. When you see something others don't, or are interested in something others are not, you move outside their sphere of awareness. It might be a certain philosophy, a love of haiku or stamp collecting, but whatever it is, your association with it puts you outside the norm. The rest of the population is immersed in the mass of mimetic desires, wanting what others want, and wanting others' desires. When you choose to spend time with others who share your odd passion, you leave the mainstream behind, head down a side stream, a less traveled way.

It can feel lonely off the beaten track, especially if people find your new perspective incomprehensible, or if they call you names for being different, or exclude you because they feel threatened by your individuality. By banding together with other wabi sabi writers, you increase the circle of solitude.

Consider a group of people who love fly-fishing. They prefer fly-fishing because it puts them in constant relationship with the elements, actively casting and moving the fly in order to lure trout from dark hiding places into the light. This focused vigilance produces strong feelings of flow and is highly satisfying. Now imagine that a fellow joins the group and listens carefully for several meetings until finally he speaks up: "I think we should spend more time dropping worms on hooks and waiting for fish to come along." After a stunned silence, one of the seasoned fly-fishers in the group says politely, "Bait fishing is not fly-fishing. We are interested in fly-fishing. We like it better."

"It seems like a lot of work," the newcomer persists.

"It is, but you are in such direct contact with nature, a part of the pattern, you are fishing, not just waiting."

"I catch my line in the bushes and get all sweaty trying to get my fly loose. Besides, I catch more fish bait-fishing."

"That might be true, but we like fly-fishing better."

"I don't see why."

Then there will be ten offers to take the newcomer out to show him, help him master the technique that will allow him to experience the joy others feel when they are fly-fishing. In a group like this, a group of friends who love the same experience, there is no need to say, "Bait fishing stinks; if I can't fly-fish, I'd rather not fish at all," because the focus is the love of fly-fishing, not the disdain of other forms of fishing.

On the other hand, there might be a group of fly-fishers who are less in love with fly-fishing itself and more in love with the prestige that goes along with fly-fishing, the elite appeal of a craft that is difficult to master. These are the sort of folk who are likely to set up fly-fishing competitions designed to keep amateurs in awe and "real" fly-fishers in positions of prestige. Exclusion and status are what these people love, not fly-fishing, though they may like that activity well enough. Such groups are made up of allies, not friends. The difference is an important one. People who have never experienced a community formed among friends will easily fall into the other pattern, dethroning the subject of attention in favor of the lesser monarch of manipulation.

Now imagine the whole process around wabi sabi and writing. A writer happens upon a book such as David Macfarlane's *Summer Gone* and mentions it to a few friends, but they seem perplexed. "No plot," one friend says. "I couldn't get into it," another confesses. Then the writer reads a book about wabi sabi and recognizes that the thing she loved about *Summer Gone* is its wabi sabi quality. This is an epiphany. She really wants to write like that. She wants to be a wabi sabi writer. Perhaps then a miracle happens and she sees a woman reading *Summer Gone* in a bookstore. She introduces herself to this woman, who turns out to be a writer.

Less miraculously and more likely, she will find a writer online or in a local writing group who has read the book, and they can discuss it and encourage each other. She will naturally form a bond with such a person. At first, there might be just two sharing the solitude, but as they find others they will form a group, and the shared identity will grow to become a community. Connecting like this is rare but not unheard of.

I worked in or managed various bookstores for more than fifteen years, and I found that people came in looking for books by writers who shared their particular view on a given subject or discussed a topic they were suddenly interested in. If I recognized what they were looking for and pointed them to the right book, they often asked me earnestly if there were others like them, others interested in studying the topic or getting together to talk about the book. When I could, I would help people connect. Independent bookstores are often run by men and women of furyu. Talk to them and ask them to call you if others express an interest in wabi sabi. Chances are that you will not be able to form a group of writers who are all interested in wabi sabi, but you never know.

The more writers you meet the more likely it will be. At the very least, you will find other writers who understand what you are trying to do. Make friends with haiku poets. Make friends with any writer who strikes you as authentic. Many of the people I have met who are interested in wabi sabi are creative people. If you are fortunate enough to connect with a group of writers who are familiar with wabi sabi, recognize how valuable it is and remember that a healthy writing community is based on friendship, not on how well each writer writes. Friendship is more important than skill or talent or even wabi sabi because friends are equals. Such communities might be very different from other groups you have been a part of. Groups of this kind don't have members as much as they have individuals. In other groups people are controlled by hierarchies, must watch their backs, watch their competition, forge alliances, avoid the wrong people and cultivate the right people, and worry about their image. These power-based groups generate fear and anxiety and squelch creativity. Some writing groups operate in this way, but the love of writing is secondary to a love of status and prestige. Focus on writing and focus on wabi sabi, make writing and wabi sabi your shared interest, rather than your shared goal.

In second-century Syria, a man named Publilius Syrus was born. As a young man he was carted off to Italy as a slave, but then he was freed by his master, given an education, and encouraged to develop his talent for acting as an *improvisatore*. "Friendship," Publilius said, "either finds or makes equals." Woodrow Wilson echoed Publilius's sentiment when he said, "You cannot be friends upon any other terms than upon the terms of equality."

The equality these men talked about is not the equality of merit because merit implies judgment, and judgment occurs when groups exist for a reason other than the love of a thing or activity. Groups based on the equality of appreciation know the full range of camaraderie and very little of the mire of status, prestige, and exclusivity. Wabi sabi groups, be they writers or otherwise, avoid excluding others. Everyone who catches the spirit of wabi sabi will enrich the group. Let the so-called "riffraff" in; they might be the wonky wabi people who inspire you with their eccentricity.

The Literary Life

To be separated from the mass of people who conform to the tastes and views of the masses, to courageously choose a community based on common interest or insight, and to write from this place is to experience that immense solitude Lewis talked about. That solitude is special, it is the solitude of sabi, and choosing it over the loud tumult of the masses is courageous. When you are feeling low and alone, come back to this page and read this quote by Anne Lamott from her book *Bird by Bird*, "There are those of us, some published, some not, who think the literary life is the loveliest one possible, this life of reading and writing and corresponding. We think this life is nearly ideal." The folks Lamott is talking about stand apart from the mass of humanity because the way of life they treasure thrives on inclusion, on sharing, on bringing many voices together. It is a life of stories and ideas. Friendship is the fabric; narrative stitches it together.

When I was twenty-five years old I discovered a group of writers like the ones Anne describes. I longed to be a part of it, but knew I never would be because it had disbanded years earlier. What that group had celebrated was, among other things, wabi sabi. C. S. Lewis was a part of it, as was J. R. R. Tolkien. Members jokingly referred to it as The Inklings, because they were writers who wrote about, among other things, moments of revelation. Lewis captured the flavor of the group when he wrote, "The pleasure of friendship is greatest when the whole group is together, each bringing out all that is best, wisest, or funniest in all the others. Those are the golden sessions when four or five of us, after a hard day's walking have come to an inn, when our slippers are on, our feet spread out towards the blaze, and our drinks at our elbows, when the whole world, and something beyond the world, opens itself to our minds as we talk, and no one has any claim on or any responsibility for another, but all are free men and equals as if we first met an hour ago while at the same time an affection, mellowed by the years, enfolds us. Life, natural life, has no better gift to give."

Lewis insists that friendship must be about something, must be two or more people walking side by side, investigating a country, an idea, a book, a topic. Friends look not at each other, but at the thing that binds them together.

If you cannot find wabi sabi writers, haijin, or others interested in the subject, then stay close to your friends who are living out the subject matter of great literature: family, romance, coming of age, loss, conflict, acceptance, maturity, insight, wisdom;

in short, anyone who is really engaged in life. Go on trips with these friends, be they literal ones or trips of the imagination. Set about a task with them, be it cleaning up a garden or weeding out bad ideas. In shouldering a coffin or shouldering responsibility they cannot bear alone, you all learn to take turns, flow in the ever-changing dynamic of friend with friend. Like workers in a foundry, take turns at the hammer, forge steel between yourselves, a resilient core of iron purified and tempered by the fire of respect, a fire that tells the truth, expresses opinions, and bares the soul.

Great community is achieved by paddling together, walking together, gardening together, fishing together, writing together, and all the while thinking and talking and also being silent to think or observe or listen. Exist in silence. Listen so well that your self vanishes through your directed attention. Always and in every situation keep handy that notebook and gently inform your friends that you are not ignoring them when you abandon a shared task for your notebook. Tell them what you have seen, what you have thought, what story idea has struck you. The artist as well as the tradesperson respects a person who attends to his or her profession and will make exceptions for your need to scribble. But be careful not to try friends' patience; note taking is capturing inspiration, not entering into flow on the spot.

I have made it a point to consider my family and friends before my calling to be a writer. It is out of my daily interactions with them that I notice the things worth writing about. Community is a conduit for ideas and images, gushing out so much material that no writer should ever complain about a lack of things to write about.

Write from the Heart

The central message of Derrick Jensen's book *A Language Older than Words* is that all of nature speaks to us. It is an idea similar to John Daido Loori's "intimate talk." In the book, Jensen describes his experience as a writing instructor. He went into his first class believing that his job was not to lead, judge, correct, or grade, but to help students to *feel* and to express their feelings through writing. Following Carl Rogers's lead, he devised a way to promote self-discovery and self-appropriated learning. On the first day of class he asked the students what they loved, encouraged them to write about it, and announced soon afterward that he was having trouble grading their work. How could he ask them to write from the heart and then assign a grade to their work? His solution was to assign grades based on how much writing was turned in, not on quality or any other measurement. This solution at first seemed to reward those who could spin out reams of words, but Jensen reasoned that participation in class would give those who wrote freely something to write about. Those who could not write freely would be stretched to do so.

To make things interesting, students were then asked to submit works composed in forms other than writing. Students brought in food, paintings, and musical compositions. One of them, a chef from Kuwait, cooked a seven-course meal and showed pictures of his country. Another student showed a video of himself rock climbing. All this was combined with lively class discussions of meaty questions. What is love? What do you want out of life? Is there such a thing as a universal good? Is the universe a friendly place or not?

The writing poured forth, Jensen cheered his students on, and then he upped the ante. He started giving his students the opportunity to develop furyu. Jensen never mentions furyu in his book, but his next actions clearly demonstrated a tangible way to develop it in a group setting. He reasoned that since experience leads to good writing, he would give marks to students every time they did something they had never done before. Students went to symphonies, rock concerts, and Vietnamese restaurants. They watched foreign films, got counseling, and connected with family members in new ways. Even unexpected or unwanted experiences were rewarded with a mark. Jensen pushed further into furyu. He felt he still had too much control over the class, so he broke it into groups and gave each group two hours to lead the class in any way they wanted.

One group wanted to play capture the flag, so the class played capture the flag, and then wrote about it. They found the experience bound them together. Another group distributed Popsicles and had the class watch cartoons and draw pictures from their childhood. Lessons in the Tush Push (a country-western dance) were followed by games of hide-and-seek in the basement of the building. Each new experience drew people out of their comfort zones and closer to each other.

Jensen didn't know it at the time, but he was building community by continually spiralling back to the question, "What do you love?" Each new experience allowed students to consider, "Did I love that? What did I or didn't I love about that?" For a final paper, his assignment was that each person must walk on water and then write about it. The slackers put a few inches of water in their bathtub and walked across, but one walked across a frozen lake, another quit smoking, another overcame her shyness and asked a man out. Another told his parents he wanted to be an artist and not an accountant.

What do you love? That question rides the wave of experiences, brings attention out, away from the self, promotes self-forgetting, and at the same time blooms inside a community drunk on furyu, finds what is real, makes contact with the real self. Furyu is a way to get past authoritarian models, be they in the classroom or in class distinctions. Equality of interest, equality of membership, equality of expression; friendship is the basis of real community. The process taught Jensen that his role as a teacher was not to control, manage, or inspire; it was to love his students. What writers want, he concluded, was to love and be loved for who we are.

Eight

Wabi Sabi Elements:
flowing words reveal constant content

IN THE WET SAND

A BEAR'S PAW PRINT

FRESH FISH IN MY CREEL

Writer: "Which elements of writing are the most wabi sabi?"

Basho: "If you make the universe your friend, aware each moment of the true nature of things—mountains and rivers, trees and grasses, and the mass of humanity—you will find all the wabi sabi elements you need."

Writer: "But which ones will impart the quality of wabi sabi most effectively?"

Basho: "Since ancient times, those who dealt with the writing brush were drawn to embellishments at the cost of content; or took content seriously, but ignored furyu."

Writer: "So furyu and content are more important than specific elements?"

Basho: "A skilled writer who has nothing to write about or is not open to beauty and enlightenment is a hollow gourd transporting water from one container to the next but never full herself. Get full, and then return to this world of ordinary humanity and write."

Writer: "What is the difference between content and elements?"

Basho: "Elements allow content to be seen."

Writer: "Where does a writer get content?"

Basho: "Go to the pine if you want to learn about the pine or go to the bamboo if you want to learn about the bamboo. And when you do, stop thinking of yourself as a poet or anything else. Poetry emerges on its own from the object when you achieve unity with it, when you dive under its surface and glimpse its hidden light. No matter how big your vocabulary is, you cannot tell the truth as long as you see yourself separate from the object. Waka was in the willow trees; haiku is in the mud snails. Each object stimulates a poetic response. It flows out of you when you become one with the object."

Ten Elements

Wabi sabi elements accentuate the content of your writing and bring out the wabi sabi depth and beauty. Here are ten elements to consider as you search for unity with your subject.

Nature

Nature includes human nature, and so is the subject of everything that is written, except for speculation about things that are not natural, like God and polyester. When Basho referred to nature, he was thinking of those powerful wilderness settings that evoke awe or wonder or a range of more subtle mental sighs.

One natural element that he insisted on was a seasonal reference. If you decide to improve your seasonal references, use descriptions to replace the actual name of the season. Instead of winter, spring, summer, autumn or fall, describe snow steaming on a horse's back, ice cracking open in the sun, a cat chasing grasshoppers in dry grass, or leaves in wind.

Each season has a mood. Use it to accentuate the tone of the content. The location will affect the seasonal feel, and you may need to go into some detail to make this clear. December in Istanbul will be different from December in Fairbanks. Devote some time to exploring seasonally correlated emotions. In my part of the world September conjures the excitement of returning to school, October the transition into winter, November the darkness and the thankfulness for the light of a warm hearth, December the building excitement of winter holidays, and so on.

Also remember the seasons of life. Children are spring, teenagers summer, adults fall, seniors winter, but avoid clichés like "the autumn of his life," and instead create phrases or descriptions that are new. Put familiar objects in a telling context. "On the edge of the dusty patio-stones lay a ruin of ripe plums and drunken wasps. He had been watching the insects, his eyes drawn to their pulsing bodies, but now, beyond them at the edge of the lake he saw his daughter, kicking her long legs at the water; at the boys." If this image works you will see, smell, and hear summer in a more engaging and interesting way than the one word could ever convey.

In *The Unknown Craftsman,* Japanese philosopher Soetsu Yanagi states that "nature depends on pattern." A writer should use natural patterns to convey truth. Seasons are one pattern, as is the life cycle of birth, growth, decline, death. But there are other patterns everywhere in nature. In the example in the previous paragraph, the drunken wasps share a condition with the playful girl. Whether fermented fruit or sensual experiences, the natural elements of summer can intoxicate. Haijin look for such patterns, which convey more than the static identification of items in the environment. Ducks flying in a V formation, the moon rising over the water, and well-pruned branches all convey more than the simple identification of the objects, more than scientific analysis. They capture something of the experience of the time of day, or the time of year, or the place. This is the great power of natural patterns. For example, a field of well-pruned grape vines creates an image in a reader's mind, and from the image the reader can deduce something about the person who owns the vines. This image and the process of deduction are more engaging than is reading "John was an experienced gardener."

Like cars, people travel along predictable routes, the patterns of boulevards and behavior. Great literature follows these routes, highlighting stages or transitions that are common to most of us. Incorporate growth in your subjects; explore maturity, oldness, experience, and wisdom. Include the history of things in their descriptions; include the lineage and life experience of a person, the events that have worn an object or building, and the details that show that time has passed.

Place

It is a curious thing that our early memories become solid with time, grow gemlike in the amber of memory. Awkward bones grow up in you as you age, bones of a different sort than the calcium ones that frame your body. These are the bones of place, refusing to break free from the past and dissolve into the present. "Place" is the skeleton on which memories hang. "Place" is the stone floor of the canyon our life etches out of the land. The place you grew up is present inside you, echoing back your calls from your present location, providing a background, a context, a stage. It might have been country fields or city streets. What was the color of the soil, the shape of the hills, the regular weather? How did you know you were home? Was it the smell of dust over the fields, the sound of a foghorn, the soft touch of a dog's muzzle? After being away, did the sight of your elementary school trigger a sabi moment?

"Place" is buried in your neural pathways. Your thoughts are made up of place references, points of measurement from which you construct your view of the world. Place pushes archetypal images into your mind as you write. Thomas Merton wrote in his diaries about the rooms he found himself living in, comparing them to his previous rooms, noticing which memories were associated with each set of rooms.

Look for the unique wabi sabi markers of a place, its geological formations, and its social expectation. What phrases do people say that give away the county or district they grew up in? Are there clothes from a former time? An old hunting vest, a classic party dress, traditional or regional garments? Quilts, crafts, folk art? There are many telling objects, some more and some less wabi sabi. Do the people of a place wear rubberized rain hats, or do they carry umbrellas? Are there sun hats or fur caps on the coat hooks? What is common and everyday, something the locals take for granted but strangers find unusual? A classic style of architecture, a nostalgic kind of car, a comfort food? Notice the things that are kept and the things that are thrown away. Notice what people put on their mantels, what they give as gifts. Notice which people have houseplants, gardens, a canoe. How far removed are they from nature, and what place does nature have in their lives?

Aloneness

To be alone in nature usually means to be without human company. Spiritual writers down through the ages have noticed the positive effect that being alone has on people. In the book *Never Cry Wolf*, Farley Mowat recounts his time spent in the wild studying wolves. Learning to survive on his own, seeing the wolves differently from others, going a little odd from lack of human contact, are all interesting results of being alone. Aloneness is different from loneliness; it is singularity, individuality, uniqueness. How a character behaves when she is alone tells a lot about her. How a subject relates to other subjects requires a process of isolating it to find its uniqueness. This shift from seeing a subject alone to seeing it in context can evoke deep thoughts and emotions.

Character

Basho's ideal of a "wabi man" is basically an educated eccentric. Bailey White's *Quite a Year for Plums* is my favorite example of intelligent, eccentric, believable characters. Passions and interests reveal the characters' eccentricity. One character is awkward amongst people but feels at home in the woods; another collects antique electric fans. I enjoy books like this because I get to know these oddballs; get to be a part of their world. David Mcfadden taught me, "If the main character puts the milk in the fridge, don't write it down, but if the main character puts the cat in the fridge, write that down." Authentic characters will be ones who act consistently throughout a story.

To achieve consistency, spend some time studying the patterns in human populations we call personality types. *Please Understand Me II* by David Keirsey or *People Patterns: A Modern Guide to the Four Temperaments* by Stephen Montgomery give readable introductions to the art of sorting people into types. Be careful how far you take this, however. Wabi sabi stresses individuality over groupings. Eccentricity will develop differently for different people depending on their personality. Show characters developing furyu, show the unpredictability of human existence, show characters who learn to flow, show characters who change.

Openness

There is a bias against closure in literary circles. Some writers insist that stories don't really begin or end, that happy endings are rare, and that the job of the writer is to tell the truth, no matter how painful. This approach has produced a good number of honest but depressing books. As indicated in earlier chapters, Basho followed furyu through sabi to karumi. Karumi allowed him to acknowledge sorrow without dwelling on it. He remained open to beauty and humor. That openness is itself attractive.

When you tell a story or expound on a subject, be careful not to close too many doors; don't tie up too many ends, don't tidy away or hide the parts you might like to ignore. If you are going to tell the truth, tell it all, but remember that wabi sabi is beyond fatalism.

Humility

Basho wrote about domestic scenes: rice planting, house cleaning, sleeping in inns. Like other poets of his day, he sought to capture the feelings associated with such ordinary activities and communicate them in a way that neither inflated nor demeaned them. He found poetic sparks in the most humble of daily events. Humility itself was admired. Real humility is worth illustrating, worth bringing to people's attention. Show the grandfather resisting his urge to give his grandson advice, show him waiting until the child asks. Show the grandmother accepting praise for her pie from the local baker. Wabi sabi is on the sensitive side of weakness, has sympathy for failing health. It shows the courage of the runt of the litter, the love of the challenged neighbor, the tempered mettle of the recovering addict.

Authenticity

There are real heroes in the world, but there are no superheroes. Whether you are writing about cooking or quantum mechanics, a novel or a manual, the wabi sabi element that will set you above other writers is authenticity. A writer who speaks in generalizations and generalities may be covering up a lack of knowledge or a lack of affection for her subject. The old adage "write what you know" is valid in this respect: if you pretend you know, your reader will find out. But it is also true that writing about a subject you know little or nothing about but are eager to learn will produce writing with a certain infectious enthusiasm. There is nothing like a new convert to excite others about a subject.

Juxtaposition

As Basho said at the beginning of Chapter 4, Soin and his "talkative forest" shared his interest in expressing *yugen*, which I will talk about in more detail in a moment. The main element that Soin and his disciples experimented with was juxtaposition. The payoff of this element is that it can produce sudden insight as dissimilar or similar images are brought together in the reader's mind. We see things differently when they are contrasted against or compared to other thing. Basho cautioned his disciples to use juxtaposition sparingly, and to avoid as much as possible its more transparent cousins—simile, metaphor, and analogy. Since Basho himself used all these to good effect, the lesson seems to be balance and sensitivity. Consider the following haiku, in which I experiment with this element:

TOUCHING THE GARDENER'S ARM
NEW CAMELLIA BUDS
HARD AS SNAILS

Technically this comparison is a simile, since a new camellia bud can have the hardness, feel, and shape of a snail. The poem works because it says more than "camellia buds are like snails." It alludes to the sudden remembrance a gardener has when she first bumps against an unseen snail eating up tender new leaves. There is a delayed sense of relief in this poem. Camellia is an early bloomer, putting out buds well before snail season, yet it foretells that the season is as certain to come as the buds are to open. The play on "hard as nails" may or may not work for the reader depending on her tolerance for cuteness.

Yugen

Have you ever entered a grove of trees and felt something that made you lower your voice? Have you looked upon a series of receding hills and longed to investigate the valleys between them? Empty parking lots, the slow compaction of newly fallen snow, a bird flying into a cloud, these things can trigger in us a pause, a stumble into adoration. The mind puzzles, "What is going on there?" Whatever it is, it's mysterious and attractive. A work of art that hints at that deep something has *yugen* (pronounced "you-gane"). Yugen rolls in distant bird calls masked by mist, sparkles in a forest of raindrops, escapes detection like a field of deer mice. It shimmers behind things, the real meaning behind words, the significance of a gift only some at the party will know. It is the deep mystery of things; the subtle profundity waiting behind the surface we see. How does a writer convey this mystery? By choosing which details to include. Certain words carry multiple meanings, but yugen is more than pillow talk, more than saying one thing to allude to another. The contemporaries of Basho described it as the darkening and intensifying of a classic ideal.

For example, I may wish to convey the loneliness and contentment you sometimes feel while walking a dog along an empty beach. Here is one way to write it: "John unclips the leash and stands alone while his dog runs away from him down the long spit of sand in the cold December dawn. When the animal reaches the end of the sand, she continues a short way into the lake, stands and barks at the water, at a passing gull, and then at the empty gray sky. With nowhere else to go, she turns and runs in long galumphing strides back down the long stretch of sand to circle her master and give a dancing exulted shake."

Here is an alternative: "John looks down the long spit of sand. On the distant point a small figure barks at a wave, a passing gull, the sky. The dog's head jerks out of sync with the sound. When the last bark reaches John, the dog is already running back fast. The thump of each paw cracks the dark rain-smoothed surface, revealing dry sand beneath. Following the path of her voice, the dog arrives, shakes, wags, and then stands looking at her master. Cool air mingles into the steam of each panting breath."

Both set of sentences contain exactly eighty-nine words. Which one contains yugen? In the second sentence the perspective shifts from an objective description of what John is seeing to a private, understated glimpse into his way of seeing. The images of the breaking sand, the dog following its voice, and the contrast between the barks and the pants, seem to take the imagination to a deeper significance in the scene. The panting of the dog at the end is more intimate, more evocative of John's state of mind. Instead of just a fond doggy moment, we have a yugen moment.

Author T. C. McLuhan deliberately weaves the image and theme of the spiral and labyrinth in her book *The Way of the Earth*. By showing the symbols in different cultures, by delving into the meaning behind the symbols, she creates a sense of yugen. Nature does this to us, repeats patterns in different ways until we notice. The echo from a braying mountain sheep, the repeated shapes of leaves stacked like scales to the top of the maple tree, the thousands of grass stalks undulating together across the prairie hills. Patterns of patterns. Each bray or leaf or stalk is one pattern that is also assembled into a second pattern, a call, a tree, or a field. You can do the same thing in your writing; pick an image and bead it through a story or article so that finally, by the end of the work, there is a lasting importance in that image, a reverberating rhythm, a layered significance, a shifting, living meaning. If the pattern is more subtle and difficult to see, it is also more enticing. By bringing together similar or dissimilar things, yugen momentarily appears. The early haiku poets advised writers wishing to achieve yugen in their work to imitate things rather than state them plainly. In the same way that certain Chinese jars were said to "move perpetually in their stillness," writing that is yugen will sometimes have a beautiful form that takes the content to that deeper level.

I glimpsed yugen one time after an evening class. As I came out the front door and turned toward the library, I saw a bicycle

leaned against a lamp pole. It was an old bicycle with aluminum
fenders and a large leather seat. It was not locked to the pole,
just leaned against it. I looked around the courtyard and there
was no one in sight. I stood for several minutes listening for footsteps, voices, anything. A small breeze came along and made rain
droplets sparkle in the lamplight. I shivered. After an hour in the
library I went home and wrote a long poem, five large stanzas, in
which I tried to capture all the details and memories that came
into my head as I thought about that bike under the lamp pole. I
have taken that poem out and tinkered with it for almost twenty
years, stripping away the intellectual speculations and the superfluous images. At the moment it looks like this:

> rain fills the dark campus
> your bicycle is leaned against a lamp pole
> over on Mt. Tolmie bushes hush into silence
> out at sea a ship rises on a long swell
>
> I enter the library
> lights hum, a page turns
> long rows of silent words
>
> I walk back into the night
> under the lamp pole
> your bicycle is gone
> but still the cone of lamp-lit rain

What I want to get across in this poem is how that bicycle seemed holy, how it revealed the pattern of other students traveling the night with me, but separate; other. I had a clear feeling of how people everywhere are going about their lives in private solitudes. When the experience reached its full extension it collapsed like a bubble, not *popping* so much as *slumping* into a drop of soapy water.

Some have suggested that symbols are a Western example of art that conveys yugen. I think rather that symbols are a metaphor for what a good piece of writing does when it expresses yugen. The story or poem is not the mystery, in the same way that the symbol is not the thing it symbolizes. The story or poem simply helps us feel the mystery, transfers the longing the writer felt into us, infects us with significance.

Once there was a king who gained important land and riches through successful military campaigns against the dark dominions that threatened his borders. He forged political alliances with men of power and influence. After securing his kingdom, he developed a thriving economy and implemented a well-designed government and legal system.

The king's greatest joy was his only son, whom he loved very much. He made sure that the boy had the latest toys, the best books, the top teachers, and the most stimulating company. Cooks prepared his favorite meals and his mother arranged elaborate parties with the most popular entertainers and important and interesting guests. A small army of tailors, shoemakers, and milliners clothed the prince in the latest fashions. When he wished to go hunting with his friends or to travel abroad, he rode the best horse or sailed the fastest ship. Strangely, however, the young man was not happy, and nothing the king could do would change his son's mood. So he called together a team of experts and asked for their advice. They deliberated for many months, and when they came back to the king, they said, "You must dress the prince in the shirt of a truly happy man, and he will be cured of his sorrow."

"Ah," thought the king, "a quest worthy of my talents," and set out immediately on a journey to find a truly happy man so that he might procure that man's shirt.

In a nearby town lived a respected priest who was known for his cheerful personality and lively wit. The priest was surprised one day to open his door and see the king standing on his doorstep. "To what do I owe this honor, your Majesty?" the priest asked after they were seated at the priest's humble fireside. "I will be frank with you," the king said. "I have heard from many people that you are a good and holy man, and I wonder if you would accept the position of Bishop, should it be offered to you." The priest, who was aware of the king's reputation for positioning key people in important places, was flattered. "Your Highness, I would certainly accept such an important position, should you offer it to me, and should the Lord see fit to place me there. I have always wanted to serve God and the King in such a position." The king smiled at the priest's well-phrased reply but continued on his way, thinking to himself, "If that man were happy, he would not be so eager for a promotion."

The king visited an old friend, who ruled a large country known for its merry people. During the royal welcoming feast, the king leaned over to his friend and said, "You seem to be a happy man. What is your secret?" The host replied to the king, "I have power and riches and I enjoy my life, but the truth is that at night I lie awake worrying that a neighboring army will invade our peaceful country and strip us of all that we hold dear." The king nodded knowingly, for he was familiar with these cares. "This man's shirt will do no better than my own," he thought.

For months, he went from city to town to village and throughout the countryside, but all those he met were not truly happy. Dejected and sad, the king finally headed home with the vague notion that he would ask his team of experts for more advice on how to find a truly happy man.

While traveling along a country road between ancient stone walls he heard a joyous song wafting on the breeze and turned his horse up a muddy lane in the direction from which the song came. In the distance, he saw a solitary farmer working in his vineyard. Drawing near, the king saw that the man's feet were bare and his tattered coat was held closed by large buttons made from sheep's horn. When the farmer looked up he smiled broadly and called out, "Good day, good day!"

The king climbed down from his horse and walked over to the man. "You seem happy today," he said.

The farmer looked at the royal pin holding the king's cape about him and replied, "Not just today; I am happy every day of the year. I am blessed with a wonderful life!" The king looked the man over, noticed his calloused hands, his patched trousers, and his ragged hat. But the man's shabby clothes dwindled into insignificance as the king rested his gaze on the farmer's smile.

The king said, "Your smile is so radiant. Come with me to the royal castle. You will be surrounded with luxury and never want for anything again."

The farmer's smile changed and he reached out and plucked a grape from a nearby vine and munched it before replying. "Thank you. You are a generous soul, but I must tell you truthfully that I would not give up my life for all the castles in the world."

The king threw his hands in the air and whooped with joy. "My son is saved! Please, you must do something for your king!"

The farmer bowed his head and said, "I am yours to command, your Majesty."

The king reached out and carefully unbuttoned the farmer's shaggy jacket, exclaiming as he did so, "Your shirt, all I want is your shirt!"

The farmer laughed but the king stared in stunned silence. All that was under the farmer's coat was the farmer's bare chest. The truly happy man was not wearing any shirt at all.

This Italian folk tale of a king's search for the source of happiness is based on the real-life story of Alexander the Great's own search. Do you have a sense of what made the farmer happy? The story does not tell you, but it hints at it. It contrasts the king and his son with the farmer. It trusts that you will deduce why the farmer is happy and the prince is not.

In Chapter 4 of this book, Basho explained that Soin used juxtaposition to hint at deeper meaning, putting two images together to surprise the reader into beauty. This story does that; it sets the king in quest of something that cannot be found. The king finds the answer to his quest in the absence of something, rather than in the presence of something.

Basho used juxtaposition himself to point to deeper meanings. Consider the following poem:

ROADSIDE WILDFLOWER
BLOOM AFTER BLOOM
IN MY HORSE'S MOUTH

Basho brings the flowers to our attention and then reveals a hidden side to them. We may appreciate their visual beauty, but the horse appreciates their taste.

Constancy and Change

Basho understood that while you explore "wind and stream" you might become overwhelmed by constant exposure to wabi sabi elements, so he developed a cognitive anchor that helps the mind adapt to the ever-changing perspective. He taught his students to look for *fueki ryuko*, which literally means "constancy and change" but which Basho used to convey the idea that within the ever-changing stream of events are recognizable and enduring patterns.

Here is an example of fueki ryuko. Except for your brain cells, 50 million of the cells in your body will have died and been replaced with others, all while you have been reading this sentence. Every second, 15 million blood cells alone are destroyed; in all, 300 million cells die in the human body every minute. The scientific community is in debate about the longevity of neurons, but there is credible speculation that each human body replaces all its cells every seven years. Every year, about 98 percent of the atoms in your body are replaced. Hold out your hand and look at it. Same scars, same wrinkles, but not the same flesh. Without your knowing it, silently and efficiently and continually, your body morphs beneath you, all the while retaining its shape; a wave of change conforming to a recognizable form.

Here is a haiku of Basho's that reflects this element:

A WILD SEA
AND ARCHING TO SADO ISLAND
THE MILKY WAY

In this poem, we have the turbulent ocean with its many white-capped waves reflected in the tranquil expanse of the Milky Way. The two vast realms resemble each other, but while the ocean is clearly in constant change, the galaxy appears eternally the same, showing itself night after night with slow and majestic patterns as predictable as any terrestrial observer would choose to name.

What do we make of Basho's poem now that we know the dynamic activity throughout the universe? Is fueki ryuko merely an illusion? The answer is enigmatic. The truth of wabi sabi is that things are constantly in motion, but that within that motion are patterns of beauty. We value the coming and going, but there is something else that makes the coming and going more interesting still. The changeable ocean always remains obedient to gravity, a constant that ensures other constants such as flow and ebb. Celestial objects in turn are obedient to galactic forces. At another level, the phenomenon of waves remains the same, even if each wave is different and even if the medium that the wave moves through changes. Likewise, because the average admirer of the night sky does not notice much coming and going from the state we call "star," she experiences a small intellectual delight when she finds that the universe is actually boiling with activity. Finally, within the constant change of the ocean and the galaxy there is the predictable but nonetheless valuable emotional reaction we call awe or humility.

By thinking about these patterns, by contemplating the changes each season brings, you begin to connect with a long view of things, a faintly noble view that what is, is, and what will be, will be. The eternal shines through the transient.

When you strive to capture a deep pattern with phrases and stories that are overused, your writing will be forgettable. You need to express the deep pattern in a new or renewed way.

Takamura Kyoshi (1874–1959), the poet who actually coined the name "haiku," said, "Deep is new." By expressing a universal value or revealing a constant pattern in an unusual or interesting way, you may actually bring the value or pattern to a whole new group of readers who would not see it in the old form.

Nine

Craft:
guidelines for developing a saving style

A TATTERED GOOSE—ONE EYE GONE

A GIRL

HOLDS OUT BREAD

When Basho neared the end of his life he dictated this poem:

SICK ON MY JOURNEY
NOW ONLY MY DREAMS WANDER
THE EMPTY FIELDS

But then some time later he could not resist editing a haiku he had written earlier and dictated:

A WHITE CHRYSANTHEMUM—
NOT A SPECK OF DUST
DISTRACTS THE EYE

These last two poems summarize Basho's life; a journey to clear sight. Why does he say that his dreams still roam the empty hills? Does this mean that even at the end of his life he still longed to wander in search of poetry? Is he saying that the moments of clarity make life in this dusty world meaningful? One thing is clear: his restless exploration of the many hills and valleys he encountered developed and honed his writing and achieved the lightness he sought. Poems from the last few years of his life are exceptionally well crafted. In them, the clever barbs of youthful wit are transmuted into piercing perceptions of wabi sabi insight. The light that shines from these needles of poetry is pure.

In Chapters 4 and 5, I described the Way of Elegance Basho followed and suggested that it was an alternative to the popular interpretation of Buddhist teaching about nonattachment. Basho saw it as a turning from egocentricity toward the real self. Central to this turning was furyu, the expansion of appreciation for beauty both in nature and in unlikely and unnoticed places.

The spiritual benefit of this path is that it allows you to remain attached to the people and things you love while developing your craft. If you follow this path and someone you love is injured or dies, you will feel deep sorrow and loss, but because you have developed your ability to see beauty, because you have opened yourself to the constant flow of things, your brain will remain balanced and you will discover other attachments rising to compensate for your loss. You will notice things to be thankful for; you will see beauty and poetry shining from the darkness. The Way of Elegance prepares you for loss and pain; it does not resolve or remove them. It is more helpful than detachment, which is really only a form of denial. If scholars like Dr. Ghose are correct, the Way of Elegance is closer to the teachings of Buddha than to the popular misunderstanding of nonattachment. The spiritual aspect of this path is inseparable from its effect on writing. If you have a healthy connection to your attachments, your writing will be authentic.

An Ocean of Attachments

Imagine that you live on Tinidril's planet, which is almost entirely covered by ocean. Imagine that the water is made up of all your attachments. You are floating in connections. Whether you know it or not, your attachments gently buoy you toward the surface. Floating across the nexus of attachment and nonattachment are huge mats of vegetation taking nutrients from the water and creating amazing gardens that roll and pitch with the waves. Those floating lands are poetry. Poetry rides across your attachments like a pliable paradise waiting to be explored. You climb out of your attachments onto the living islands of poetry. Poetry saves you from drowning in your attachments, provides a way of living on the ocean, always near the water but able to occasionally stand above it. Imagine yourself sitting on the edge of poetry with your legs dangling into your attachments. This analogy is not far from what Basho had in mind.

Two Schools

About writing, Basho wrote, "There are two ways: one is entirely natural, in which the poem is born from within itself; the other way is to make it through the mastery of the technique." (*Narrow Road to the Interior and Other Writings* by Matsuo Basho, translated by Sam Hamill. See Appendix A.) Here, Basho contrasts his own way of writing to those of the popular schools of his day. He came into a world in which poets squabbled over the role of poetry and how poetry should be written.

One school said the old conventions were sanctimonious and prim. They ridiculed the old poems and wrote raunchy parodies of them. The other major school sought to retain something of the old master's elegance but experimented with ways to push the tired forms into something new. A great deal of the first school's effort was spent on clever innuendo and bawdy mimicry, while the second school spent its time tweaking old images and playing with a variety of techniques and styles. After participating in poetry competitions and debates about the merits of these approaches, Basho realized that both were inauthentic. The manipulation of words for effect was less like poetry and more like completing a puzzle. If you make a concerted effort to follow Basho's advice, you will find a wealth of original poetry rising within you. When that happens, you will craft something beautiful.

Fuga

The phrase "Way of Elegance" comes from two Japanese words: *michi* (way or path) and *fuga* (the elegance of poetry). Fuga is further made up of two root words. *Fu* can mean either "wind," as in furyu, or "folkways," which is its meaning in fuga. Fu in this second sense refers to the habits and manners of the common folk. As a classification for songs in China, it meant "widespread" or "well known." *Ga,* on the other hand, refers to the grace or gracefulness of ceremonies at court. It is not so much about wealth or grandeur as it is about the qualities of a poet who is well trained and broadly educated. It might be most accurately translated into English as "cultured" or "civilized." The renowned court poets were primarily interested in expressing ga through idealized and romanticized images. Thus, ga is sometimes thought of as artistic and spiritual purity.

With this in mind, we might translate *fuga* as "common ways with grace," or "blue-jean-clad eloquence," or even "spiritual art grounded in reality." The paradoxical nature of this word is what makes it useful. Think of the farm boy who goes to college and receives an advanced degree in literature. His early life with the animals and hard labor on the farm ground his later education, which is furyu because it exposes him to all sorts of things he would not experience on the farm. If he can retain fu from his life on the farm while at the same time gaining ga from his education, he will be fuga, a common man with an educated appreciation for art and culture, perhaps with spiritual insight. He will have followed the Way of Elegance.

Hideaki Hirano, Professor Emeritus at Hosei University, writes: "A man has to live in Fu, that is, in daily folkways. Can he then forget about Ga, that is nobleness of mind and pure spirituality? Or, should and could a man seek merely Ga in sacrifice to Fu? Most definitely not! When you read carefully Basho's works, including *Oku no Hosomichi (Narrow Road to the Deep Interior)*, you would agree that he devoted his entire life to this contradictory, difficult, yet important issue."

Basho wrote, "The ever changing nature of fuga changes together with heaven and earth. One respects the fact that the changes are never exhausted. The changes of heaven and earth are the seeds of poetry." (Translation from *Early Modern Japanese Literature*, edited by Haruo Shirane. See Appendix A.) A writer who follows the Way of Elegance will wander like Basho did, ever exposed to change, always uncovering in herself fertile ground for the seeds of poetry.

To use a different analogy, the turbulent waters of furyu erode the rocks of preconception and collect gold at the stream's low points. This process teaches you that when things seem darkest, there is often a gleam pointing the way to the gold. If a writer lives the Way of Elegance, her craft will develop not in spite of but because of this natural erosion. And as preconceptions are washed away, poetry is revealed. When the bright metal of poetry is at hand, other metals are set aside. Basho let harsh or crass expression fall away, let all the nonessentials fall away. If you follow his example you will create fuga stories, poems, and essays that flow from within your unity with the subject.

Shasei

Shasei literally means "sketch from life." The idea is to depict, in a few quick strokes, a thing just as it is. Close your eyes and think about your subject. Imagine that you have sketched a scene. What are the broad bones of the scene, what is crucial to know, what makes you feel that you are there, you have arrived? Start with realism and then let the poetry bubble up from what is real.

In the West we might say, "Look at it objectively." Show the details, point the eye in a direction, hold up two things together, allude, imply, and suggest, but do not presume; sketch what is there. Instead of saying, "She was miserable in the rain," say, "The rain soaked through her cap, which became heavy and cold. Water ran away from it in trickles down her face." Retain objectivity but also work for brevity. The reason this works is that it respects the reader's ability to feel an emotion. It evokes imagination to do the job and allows the reader to sympathize with the characters in a story, because imagination has created the sensations from the unbiased description of the character.

William Carlos Williams said, "All art is necessarily objective. It doesn't declaim or explain, it presents." Critics have pointed out that Williams's most famous poem does not, by this definition, qualify as art. The poem reads:

so much depends
upon

a red wheel
barrow

glazed with rain
water

beside the white
chickens.

What the critics object to is the first stanza. Without it, the poem presents an image that the reader can take in and judge for herself. What the first line does is clue the reader in to the author's sense of what is important. It makes the poem a sermon. It preaches wabi sabi instead of showing wabi sabi. Yet long before I ever knew about wabi sabi, I read and loved this poem and said to myself, "Yes, I get what Williams is saying; there is something really important about that image." Some works are closer and some are farther away from wabi sabi, and some writers have progressed further along in furyu. I accept Williams's poem as an honest expression of his own sensitivity to beauty. No act of writing is truly objective; even the selecting of images is biased. Williams knew that objectivity was important, but he demonstrated in his own writing that it is affected by the poet's choice of what to present. This technique of selective objectivity is haiku.

Haiku

One writer at the haiku meeting I described earlier said to me, "The better you get at haiku, the better your other writing gets." Another writer added that this was because haiku is "all craft." On the Way of Elegance, important moments bud out into your awareness. Your attention is like sunlight: It warms the bud, causing it to open into a flower. The fruit that grows from the flower is the poem on the page. The rules that surround haiku are the trellis, wire, and husbandry that prepare the fruit for easy picking by the reader.

Here are two poems to illustrate haiku and its rules. The first is one I wrote last week:

SEVEN SPRINGS RANCH
MY FIRST VISIT
TO HIS MEMORIES

This poem is a *senryu*, which is a poem that follows all the same rules as a haiku but focuses on a humorous image or something deeply human. To keep senryu straight from haiku I say, "Haiku describe nature and senryu describe human nature."

The second poem, which is also a senryu, was written anonymously in Japan many years ago:

LOST CHILD FOUND
THE FATHER GIVES THANKS
IN A HOARSE VOICE

Key Haiku Rules

Use fewer than seventeen syllables in one to three lines. Twelve to fourteen syllables seems to be the accepted "best length" for an English-language haiku. Both poems above are fourteen syllables.

Make the haiku in two parts—one to set the scene (Seven Springs Ranch/finding of the lost child), **and the other to describe the moment** (the sense of closeness to my friend/

the sense of relief at finding the child). It is best if the two parts are naturally separated by a break in the syntax or change in focus.

Use a seasonal reference or natural setting. There is no seasonal reference in either of these poems, but "ranch" qualifies as a natural setting, and presumably the father received his hoarse voice from calling for his child out of doors.

Show, don't tell—avoid explanation, commentary, moralizing, teaching, and so on. To make my poem obey this rule I would have to show my friend with something that related to his fond memories at the ranch. If I were able to do that, it would probably be a better poem. I found the switch from the expected location (the ranch) to the unexpected location (his memories) interesting enough by itself, but here I am open to the same criticism that was levelled at the William Carlos Williams poem. The anonymous poem adheres to this rule completely.

Use concrete, simple descriptions—focus on an object or occurrence, not on your own perception or idea about that object or occurrence. My poem breaks this rule, but the anonymous poem is very concrete and still manages to be poignant.

Use the present tense. Both poems obey this rule.

Juxtapose images if the subject warrants it. This is what makes my poem work. You are expecting me to visit a location and instead I visit a memory. The anonymous poem does not contain juxtaposition, but it does combine two images to tell more than any one of the images would alone.

Avoid pronouns and speaking in the first person. I could have removed myself from the poem by simply deleting the word "my" in the second line, but when I tried that, it seemed too detached. The anonymous poem is in the third person and uses no pronouns.

Don't personify animals or other natural objects. Neither of the poems does this.

Try to end with a noun. Both poems do.

You might wonder why I included my poem when it breaks so many of the key rules. I did it to make a point. The most important thing a haiku does is convey the moment in a way that allows the reader to experience the same tickling sensation of awe, wonder, or humor that the author experienced. Basho said, "Haiku is simply what is happening in this place at this moment." He also said, "Learn the rules, then move beyond them." Here are two of his haiku that break important rules but still work well:

FROM DEEP WITHIN
THE PEONY PISTILS, WITHDRAWING
REGRETFULLY, THE BEE

This is a long poem—nineteen syllables in English. Yet this translation from *Early Modern Japanese Literature* works well because the words "withdrawing" and "regretfully" slow down the poem and imitate the reluctance the bee seems to have at leaving the flower. This poem also moves dangerously close to personification of the bee:

WITH DEWDROPS DRIPPING,
I WISH SOMEHOW I COULD WASH
THIS PERISHING WORLD

This translation by Sam Hamill captures well the feeling of looking at a fresh morning scene bedecked in a multitude of dewdrops, but the poem is largely about the poet's inner desire to freshen the world of humanity with beauty found in nature. This English translation does not specify the season, though spring is implied. Also, aside from the dewdrops, the language is largely abstract. Like William Carlos Williams's poem above, Basho is telling us something. He wants us to know that nature renews itself each day and seems to imply, "Wouldn't it be nice if human company had a similar daily cleansing?"

Haiku rules, like the rules of punctuation and grammar, help you express yourself in such a way that a reader will have the best

chance to "get it." These rules have been tried and found successful for generations. Apply the third, fourth, fifth, seventh, and
ninth rules to all your writing, and it will improve.

Poetry Beyond Verse

The book *Fugitive Pieces* begins with a stunning description
unparalleled in recent prose. The text alternates between evocative images and statements of deep insight. We see a Jewish boy
emerge from the mud where he hid from Nazi soldiers. Then we
read, "No one is born just once. If you're lucky you'll emerge
again in someone's arms; or unlucky wake when the long tail
of terror brushes the inside of your skull." This boy goes on to
experience other rebirths as he explores his attachment to different characters. The book is filled with objective details about
the boy's life with his new father and poetic interjections into the
narrative that seem to glow between the details.

Reading poetry for long periods of time can be difficult. Most
readers want order and predictable patterns. The juxtapositions,
sudden shifts, and disconnected images of poetry demand energy
from a reader. By combining a familiar narrative form (the novel)
with a more challenging but also more rewarding form (poetry),
a writer can carry a reader off the beaten track into meadows she
might never travel to on her own. Surveys that ask about people's
reading habits reveal that poetry is read by only a small percent-
age of the population, and the poetry read most often is written
by the great masters, most of whom are dead. Contemporary

poetry is read almost exclusively by other poets, an enthusiastic but small audience.

By taking her poetry into a novel, Anne Michaels became a multi-award-winning author and *Fugitive Pieces* became an international bestseller. Thousands enjoyed it who had not and would not read her poetry. In Canada, the book was number one on the *Globe & Mail's* National Bestseller List and stayed on the list for more than two years. If you want to see how a master poet of today effectively combines poetry with narrative, you will find no better example.

Michaels's style is achieved through the use of clear haiku-like sentences that regularly contain a twist or poetic turn. When the soldiers burst into his house, the boy was hidden in a wall. He describes the sounds of his parents being killed, and then silence. "My mother had been sewing a button on my shirt. She kept her buttons in a chipped saucer. I heard the rim of the saucer in circles on the floor. I heard the spray of buttons, little white teeth." There is no resorting to adjectives, no overworked metaphors, just those two sounds, the circular descending notes of the saucer and the high fragile sound of the buttons, transformed by metaphor into teeth. That sound mirrors the shattering of his psyche, represents his childhood overturned and emptied. It would be a powerful image without the metaphor, but those hard human pieces rattling free from a body begin the book with a level of emotion I at first did not believe the author could maintain—but she did. Later in the story, when silverware crashes to the floor, there is an echo of the old fear, but it is transformed by another character, who deliberately dumps her own silverware onto the floor in an act of solidarity and attachment.

Michaels shows us the pain of loss but also the beauty of attachment. She shows that attachment doesn't have to lead to pain; it can mature into unconditional love. She reveals that self-discovery and then loss of self-consciousness is part of the process.

Karumi

It took Basho most of his life to develop a style that did what he wanted, that ran along the surface of images and then dove off. Wingless, weightless, it had a lightness that floated past the usual patterns of language into poetry and past poetry into awakening. That lightness was *karumi*. Writers have been following his example for hundreds of years.

A contemporary book that echoes Basho's style is *Summer Gone* by David Macfarlane. Reviews of this title are mixed. Criticism of it has focused on the author's refusal to tell a straight story, so in one sense it is a bit like Soin's poems. It avoids saying too much, and it plays with the bones of narrative. The plot line is fractured, normal structure is left out, and there is an unconventional ending. These characteristics, for those of us who like the book, add to its appeal. It isn't that fractured plot lines are great in and of themselves, but that by arranging narrative elements in a certain way, the book opens up and gives us what we need in a way that helps us see past sequential accuracy to the true subject of the story—in this case, summer.

One of the main character's dilemmas is that he works as the editor of a magazine he finds disappointing and almost contemptible. "His skills were becoming a more valuable commodity than his notion, outdated and fast becoming antique, of the importance of good writing and precise grammar and graceful turns of phrase. His problem was that he never saw the real center of commerce: the value of overpasses, the profit of malls, the dividends of industrial parks, the wealth of apartment towers, the bonanza of subdivision, the riches of hamburgers and pizzas and tacos. He had always imagined a more genteel downtown of beautiful words and interesting, smart, unabridged ideas." This description reveals a wabi sabi man who rejects the values of commerce in favor of beauty and who values precise and clear expression in the service of grand ideas.

The book mirrors this sensibility by being both precise and about a large idea, the idea of summer. The story continually and faithfully returns to this character's thoughts and feelings about the season, the bits and pieces that matter, that create a lifetime of longing. The longing is for space, for time, for wabi sabi, for what is beyond wabi sabi. The book is filled with details, piled on one after the other, but carefully piled, like the stones of an Inukshuk, like the sticks and twigs of a hot fire, allowing air to flow in, allowing the fuel to collapse into flame.

The book progresses in this way, presenting moment after moment of precise and well-crafted descriptions that ignite memories and longings of our own. Macfarlane also repeats several moments in the story from slightly different perspectives, echoing one moment in greater detail each time, like some strange amplification of small clicks and pops in the song of an insect, revealing a depth possible only with language. These are the crickets of the book, chirping out their wabi sabi song.

By telling and then later retelling a detail, Macfarlane is able to rotate it into a different light, remind us that this is worth looking at again, like a view of the beach is worth looking at again, like that last look we take when we have packed up everything and are heading home. That last look again, and then again. Deliberate acts of remembrance. And that is what the book reads like. It is as if the best moments of a summer, the sorted and well-chosen moments, are shown to us in the context of sweet private appreciation, an affair with water, sun, camp, canoes, with the body of a season. We are presented with first the ribs, then the lungs, the chest, the heart, and finally as if assembling herself out of these components, a living, breathing personification of a summer. By giving us this slow build-up of details, this fond compilation of choice memories, we glimpse, perhaps through our own experience with the same elements in our own summers past, perhaps in the assembled stones of memory and imagination, a whole total transcendent summer beyond all summers. And the effect is that we feel the longing that the character feels, we feel a part of a community of aficionados, we feel the love both of summer places and of seasonal changes, and we feel camaraderie with the writer and all the readers who get it, who long with us for something as fragile and fleeting as the appreciation of a removal of time from memory.

It is a book that carefully and deliberately includes wabi sabi elements at the heart of the writing, whether the author knows about wabi sabi or not. The only flowery language is about flowers. The author works hard, sweats out the difficult job of the long way, the canoe portage of writing. He presents beauty one image at a time; he paints the story one clear and precise sentence after another. This sort of writing cannot be easy. It shows and doesn't tell, it repeats observations for us: "Bay noticed . . ." "Lark saw . . ." "Sara pointed out . . ." Detached in places, giving us distance, it also comes in close, as intimate as breath.

Unlike some purists of minimalist literature, Macfarlane does use analogy. When describing a child's perception of the tensions and uncertainty around a difficult pregnancy he says, "That May, words flew around the house. They seemed all wrong to Bay. He felt like a cage of crows had been released indoors. The strange black nouns flapped madly around the Scandinavian living-room furniture, cawed over the vinyl-covered kitchen stools, scratched their talons into the pale veneer of the bedside tables: bleeding, placenta, uterine wall, oxygen deprivation, brain damage." In the hands of a lesser writer this analogy might falter, but the sudden use of the word "bleeding," followed by the other graphic and revealing words, rescues the image and shifts it into a powerful emotional passage.

Against this image of words evoking fear in the child, we have a depiction of a camp director who is stable and unruffled—a sort of naturally evolved Zen Master made clear by his lack of self-awareness. Understated and slightly sketched, we feel the man as much as we see him. His voice is captured in a few words. Bay finds him standing near the shore looking at a speed-boat, seeing in it the end of something.

The camp director believes that by learning to paddle a canoe, and by sitting around a fire, and by other acts of routine interaction with nature, camp gives boys a liturgy, and the staff become priests. In the indoctrination to this ethic, in the unnamed ethic related to wabi sabi, this writer pushes the characters past the fear of death, to the gritty, real absence of life. But the writer doesn't stop there; he adds a third layer, a short talk by the camp director as simple as a koan, as subtle as a poem, in which he points out the disappearance of leopard frogs, painted turtles, and milk snakes in the environment around the camp. This gradual erosion of life is due, we assume, to pollution and people and the camp itself. The boys are asked by the director to "think about what nothing means. I want you to try. To think of what happens when something that once was, ceases to be. Extinction. When something is gone. For eternity."

MacFarlane describes the main character's perception of the director: "Often, after supper, Bay saw him, standing on the point outside his cabin, the smoke of a cigarette curling up into the still air. The director was looking across the water. He was listening to the fall of the evening, watching the shifts in the dusk. It was understood—without the director even saying so—that what the boys at the camp were expected to learn from him was how to pay attention to what he was paying attention to." The director's motto, inexplicable to many of the boys and never told to them, but painted on a rafter in the dining room, is "summer is the stillness between things." When I read those words, in the context of this quiet man watching the night, noticing the stillness between things, I understood that this book was a rolling echo of that central message. Every other word in the book hung on that simple yet profound motto. This was the layer of the story that explained the others. The stillness between things is so deep and so subtle that the book itself pales in comparison. All the other words live and breathe only because of those central words.

A Series of Astonishments

Fugitive Pieces and *Summer Gone* are two of the best examples of the kind of writing E. M. Forster described when he said, "Good writing is administering a series of astonishments." Sven Birkerts, writing in the January/February 2003 issue of *Book* magazine, encouraged readers to invest effort in reading Annie Proulx's book *That Old Ace in the Hole* because "the prose may be slow and demand care from the reader, but repays our attention with a thousand shocks of charged recognition." These well-crafted books provide astonishment and charged recognition because they have removed the unnecessary fabric to reveal the naked truth. There is a paradoxical density of images expressed with careful precision. Every word counts, as if each one has been weighed to make sure it will stay on the page.

In order to winnow, you must first harvest. This means that after you have immersed yourself in a subject, after you have taken the plunge and gathered the gold from the deep pools, after you have spun out miles of words, you must sit down and start to prune. In bonsai we encourage the tree to thrive, to throw out lots and lots of leaves and branches, and then we trim and cut away what is in the wrong place, or wire into shape the branches that we like but which need to be adjusted. While you are writing, explore the elements from Chapter 8, and do not stop the images and wild combinations your subconscious brings to light. The more furyu you experience, the more sensations and settings will flow out. Let it all out. Let it spring up like a bonsai full of leaves and branches and possibility. Once you have that tree, start to prune.

Well-Pruned Sentences

Have a look at *The Shipping News* for well-pruned sentences. Early in the book, Proulx describes how the main character, Quoyle, because of his job as a journalist, began to see the world as a series of news headlines. Now, as he arrives to pick up his children from his friend's house, we get a vivid glimpse into a family that Quoyle loves: "The hill tilting toward the water, the straggled pickets and then Dennis's aquamarine house with a picture window toward the street. Quoyle pulled pens from his shirt, put them on the dashboard before he went in. For pens got in the way. The door opened into the kitchen. Quoyle stepped around and over children. In the living room, under a tinted photograph of two stout women lolling in ferns, Dennis slouched on leopard-print sofa cushions, watched the fishery news. On each side of him crocheted pillows in rainbows and squares. Carpenter At Home."

This description aligns details in a narrowing cascade from the street, to the house, to the living room, to Dennis framed by two handmade cushions. Look back over the sentences and see if something could be left out. Each word is necessary. Not, "Quoyle pulled the pens from his shirt pocket," but just, "Quoyle pulled pens from his shirt." Proulx has clipped away the words that don't matter and kept the ones that do, the ones that convey the most information, and then she sums it all up with the headline, "Carpenter At Home."

I hope the examples in this chapter encourage you to examine your writing with a bonsai master's eye. The Way of Elegance plunges you into the objects and attachments you love. Unity with these things triggers a rush of poetry like abundant growth on a healthy bonsai tree, and the practice of writing haiku sharpens your pruning skills so that your writing will grow into a masterpiece of wabi sabi beauty.

May you wander yugen hills, thrive in the literary life, and hear the tenth goose in wabi sabi places.

Appendix A
Paraphrases

Unless otherwise noted, the Japanese poems and quotes from Basho's writings that appear in this book have been paraphrased in English by the author after an extensive study of each poem or passage in transliteration, translation, and exposition. They are not translations from the original Japanese. Following are the major works that were referenced:

Beilenson, Peter, trans. *A Little Treasury of Haiku* (New York: Avenel, 1980).

Bownas, Geoffrey, and Anthony Thwaite, trans. *The Penguin Book of Japanese Verse* (Baltimore: Penguin Books, 1964).

Hamill, Sam, trans. *The Sound of Water* (Boston: Shambhala Publications, Inc., 1995).

Henderson, Harold G., ed. and trans. *An Introduction to Haiku* (Garden City, NY: Doubleday, 1958).

Matsuo, Basho. *Narrow Road to the Interior and Other Writings*, trans. Sam Hamill (Boston: Shambhala Publications, Inc., 1998).

Sato, Hiroaki, and Burton Watson, ed. and trans. *From the Country of Eight Islands: An Anthology of Japanese Poetry* (New York: Columbia University Press, 1986).

Shirane, Haruo, ed. *Early Modern Japanese Literature: An Anthology, 1600–1900* (New York: Columbia University Press, 2002).

Suzuki, Daisetz T. *Zen and Japanese Culture* (Princeton, NJ: Princeton University Press, 1970).

Ueda, Makoto. *Basho and His Interpreters: Selected Hokku with Commentary* (Stanford, CA: Stanford University Press, 1991).

Yuasa, Nobuyuki, trans. *The Narrow Road to the Deep North* (London: Penguin Books, 1966).

Suggested Reading

Wabi Sabi Fiction

- *Summer Gone*, by David Macfarlane
- *Fugitive Pieces*, by Anne Michaels
- *Unless*, by Carol Shields
- *Shipping News*, by E. Annie Proulx
- *Quite A Year for Plums*, by Bailey White
- *A River Runs Through It*, by Norman Maclean
- *The Curious Incident of the Dog in the Night-Time*, by Mark Haddon
- *Perelandra*, by C. S. Lewis
- *Howard's End*, by E. M. Forster
- *Snow Falling on Cedars*, by David Guterson
- *The Bonesetter's Daughter*, by Amy Tan
- *Book of Sorrows*, by Walter Wangerin
- *Silas Marner*, by George Eliot
- *David Copperfield*, by Charles Dickens
- *The Entrance to Porlock*, by Frederick Buechner
- *The Remains of the Day*, by Kazuo Ishiguro
- *That Old Ace in the Hole*, by E. Annie Proulx
- *Rockbound*, by Frank Parker Day
- *Precious Time*, by Erica James
- *The Skull Mantra*, by Eliot Pattison

Wabi Sabi Nonfiction

- *For the Time Being*, by Annie Dillard
- *Zen and the Art of Motorcycle Maintenance*, by Robert M. Pirsig
- *Walden*, by Henry David Thoreau
- *Thomas Merton Reader*, edited by Thomas P. McDonnell
- *The Cincinnati Arch: Learning from Nature in the City*, by John Tallmadge
- *The Complete Letters of Van Gogh: With Reproductions of All the Drawings in the Correspondence*, by Vincent Van Gogh
- *A Trip Around Lake Ontario*, by David McFadden
- *A Walk Through the Year*, by Edwin and Nellie Teale
- *The Snow Leopard*, by Peter Matthiessen
- *The Sacred Depths of Nature*, by Ursula Goodenough
- *Walking the High Ridge: Life as Field Trip*, by Robert Michael Pyle
- *Pilgrim at Tinker Creek*, by Annie Dillard
- *The Practice of the Wild*: Essays, by Gary Snyder
- *Brothers and Friends: The Diaries of Major Warren Hamilton Lewis*, by W. H. Lewis
- *Romance of the Word: One Man's Love Affair with Theology*, by Robert Farrar Capon
- *Never Cry Wolf*, by Farley Mowat
- *Reason for Hope: A Spiritual Journey*, by Jane Goodall
- *On the Road* and *The Dharma Bums*, by Jack Kerouac

- *The Barn at the End of the World: The Apprenticeship of a Quaker, Buddhist Shepherd*, by Mary Rose O'Reilley

Books about Basho, Haiku, and the Way of Elegance

- *Narrow Road to the Interior and Other Writings by Matsuo Basho*, translated by Sam Hamill
- *The Narrow Road to Oku by Basho*, translated by Donald Keene
- *Basho and His Interpreters: Selected Hokku with Commentary*, by Makoto Ueda
- *Early Modern Japanese Literature*, edited by Haruo Shirane
- *Narrow Road to the Deep North and Other Travel Sketches by Matsuo Basho*, translated by Nobuyuki Yuasa
- *Haiku: This Other World*, by Richard Wright
- *Seeds from the Birch Tree: Writing Haiku and the Spiritual Journey*, by Clark Strand
- *Writing and Enjoying Haiku: A Hands-on Guide*, by Jane Reichhold
- *The Haiku Anthology*, by Cor van den Heuvel
- *Global Haiku: Twenty-Five Poets World-Wide*, edited by George Swede and Randy Brooks
- *Japanese Haiku: 220 Examples of Seventeen-Syllable Poems by Basho, Buson, Issa, Shiki, Sokan, Kikaku*, translated by Peter Beilenson
- *A Language Older Than Words*, by Derrick Jensen

- *Long Quiet Highway*, by Natalie Goldberg
- *How to Haiku: A Writer's Guide to Haiku and Related Forms*, by Bruce Ross
- *Mountain Tasting: Zen Haiku by Santoka Taneda*, translated by John Stevens
- *Chiyo-Ni: Woman Haiku Master*, by Patricia Donegan and Yoshie Ishibashi
- *Haiku Moment: An Anthology of Contemporary North American Haiku*, edited by Bruce Ross
- *The Japanese Have a Word for It: The Complete Guide to Japanese Thought and Culture*, by Boye Lafayette De Mente
- *Take a Deep Breath: The Haiku Way to Inner Peace*, by Sylvia Forges-Ryan and Edward Ryan
- *A Glimpse of Red: The Red Moon Anthology of English-Language Haiku*, edited by Jim Kacian

Books about Wabi Sabi and Related Subjects

- *Wabi Sabi Simple*, by Richard R. Powell
- *Wabi Sabi for Artists, Designers, Poets & Philosophers*, by Leonard Koren
- *Wabi Sabi: The Japanese Art of Impermanence*, by Andrew Juniper
- *Tao te ching*, by Lao Tsu, translated by Gia-Fu Feng and Jane English
- *The Book of Tea*, by Okakura and Kakuzo

- *Way of Chuang Tzu*, by Thomas Merton
- *Zen Mind, Beginner's Mind*, by Shunryu Suzuki
- *The Unknown Craftsman: A Japanese Insight into Beauty*, by Soetsu Yanagi
- *Buddhism Plain and Simple*, by Steve Hagen
- *Washi, the World of Japanese Paper*, by Sukey Hughes
- *Words in Context: A Japanese Perspective on Language and Culture*, by Takao Suzuki
- *Zen and Japanese Culture*, by Daisetz T. Suzuki
- *The Tao of Pooh*, by Benjamin Hoff
- *The Cultural Creatives: How 50 Million People Are Changing the World*, by Paul H. Ray
- *The Girard Reader*, by René Girard
- *The Way of the Earth*, by T. C. McLuhan
- *The New Drawing on the Right Side of the Brain*, by Betty Edwards
- *The Art of Living*, by Epictetus, interpreted by Sharon Lebell
- *Blink: The Power of Thinking Without Thinking*, by Malcolm Gladwell
- *In Praise of Slow: How a Worldwide Movement Is Challenging the Cult of Speed*, by Carl Honore

Aware: Sensitivity or emotional receptivity.

Fueki ryuko: Basho used this phrase to convey the idea that within the ever-changing stream of events are recognizable and enduring patterns.

Fuga: The elegance of poetry. Fuga is made up of two root words: *fu*, which means the habits and manners of the common folk, and *ga*, which refers to the grace or gracefulness of ceremonies at court.

Furyu: Literally "wind and stream" or "in the way of the wind and stream." A way of living that gradually expands a person's sense of beauty, taste, and aesthetic appreciation.

Ga: Literally "elegance." Any art that was given the designation "ga" was considered to be of the highest caliber and officially recognized by society.

Ginko: A walk in nature for inspiration.

Hade: The beauty of youth, the beauty of singers, actors, and performers. It is the beauty furthest from wabi sabi.

Haibun: Haibun in a broader sense existed before Basho in the form of prefaces, notes accompanying hokku, and short essays written by haiku masters. Basho coined the word *haibun*. It is the extrapolation of Basho's haibun form that provides the theoretical underpinnings for this book.

Haijin: A writer of haiku or someone adept at seeing haiku moments; a haiku person.

Hokku: The first verse in renga sessions, similar in structure to the first three lines of a tanka.

Iki: Literally "something that is pure, like a plant essence." A stylish sophisticated beauty with a processed sort of purity. It came to refer to refined manners and appearance.

Jimi: The beauty of sober colors, traditional treatments, and correct style.

Karumi: The hallmark of Basho's mature style. Karumi literally means a "light beauty with subtlety." When asked to describe karumi, Basho said it was a "shallow river over a sandy bed."

Ku: A division in Japanese poetry, delimited by "on" count (see below) or syntax. Usually, although not always, 5 or 7 "on."

Mono no aware: Literally "sensitivity to things." Motoori Norinaga (1730–1801) carefully scrutinized the 4,500 poems in the classic text *Collection of Myriad Leaves* made at the beginning of the Heian period and concluded that the quality unifying these poems was a sensitivity to things in nature and the transient beauty of such things.

On (sometimes referred to as Onji): The Japanese equivalent of English syllables; "on" are even shorter language units.

Renga: A form of Japanese poetry written by two or more people in which each person contributes one or more verses that are linked thematically or by a sequence of images.

Sabi: Describes the lovely lonely mood or melancholy feeling we have when we see a thing for what it is, see the flow of nature around us. Sometimes sabi refers simply to age and deterioration.

Senryu: Literally "river willow." A humorous, satiric, or insightful poem dealing with human nature, usually written in the same form as haiku.

Shibui: Literally "astringent." A kind of beauty recognized by its ability to evoke a feeling of tranquility. Shibui is marked by three main characteristics: wabi, sabi, and yugen (see below).

Tanka: Literally "short poem." A lyric poem with a five-seven-five-seven-seven pattern of syllables.

Wabi: Literally "poverty." Wabi has come to mean freedom from the distractions of affluence, freedom from the glut of possessions, and release into appreciation of simpler things.

Waka: Literally a "Japanese poem." A general term used primarily to refer to tanka and the early poetry of the Heian period.

Way of Elegance: From two Japanese words: *michi* (way or path) and *fuga* (the elegance of poetry). The elegance referred to in this phrase involves a combination of courtly grace and rural charm.

Yugen: Refers to a deep mystery behind or beneath things; it often is the substance of a haiku moment.

Credits

p. 26
The linked verses by Sodan, Chinseki, and Basho are from "Basho and Linked Poems" in Christopher Edgar and Ron Padgett, editors, _Classic in the Classroom: Using Great Literature to Teach Writing_, published by Teachers and Writers Collaborative, copyright © 1999 by Teachers & Writers Collaborative. Used by permission of the translator, William J. Higginson.

p. 69
Copyright © 1998 by Ellen Wright
Reprinted from *Haiku: This Other World* by Richard Wright, Published by Arcade Publishing, New York, New York.

p. 71
From BOOK OF HAIKUS by Jack Kerouac, edited by Regina Weinreich, copyright © 2003 by the Estate of Stella Kerouac, John Sampas, Literary Representative. Used by permission of Penguin, a division of Penguin Group (USA) Inc.

p. 172
By William Carlos Williams, from COLLECTED POEMS: 1909-1939, VOLUME I, copyright © 1938 by New Directions Publishing Corp. Reprinted by permission of New Directions Publishing Corp.

p. 177

From *The Sound of Water*, translated by Sam Hamill, © 1995. Reprinted by arrangement with Shambhala Publications, Inc., Boston, *www.shambhala.com*.

p. 177

From *Early Modern Japanese Literature* by Hurauo Shirance. Copyright © 2002 Columbia University Press. Reprinted with permissions of the publisher.